Ancient Peoples and Places

THE
EGYPTIANS

General Editor

DR GLYN DANIEL

Ancient Peoples and Places

THE
EGYPTIANS

Cyril Aldred

82 PHOTOGRAPHS
50 LINE DRAWINGS
8 TABLES
AND 2 MAPS

FREDERICK A. PRAEGER, *Publisher*

New York

THIS IS VOLUME EIGHTEEN IN THE SERIES

Ancient Peoples and Places

GENERAL EDITOR: DR GLYN DANIEL

BOOKS THAT MATTER

Published in the United States of America
in 1961 by Frederick A. Praeger, Inc., Publishers
64 University Place, New York 3, N.Y.
All rights reserved
© Thames and Hudson, London, 1961
Library of Congress catalog card number 61-5253
Printed in Great Britain by Jarrold and Sons, Ltd., Norwich

CONTENTS

19071

5

ILLUSTRATIONS

CHRONOLOGICAL TABLES

To write adequately of the Ancient Egyptians, whose ancient memorials far outnumber those of the other nations of Antiquity, within the limits of a single volume in this series, would be an undertaking for the foolhardy or the overweening. I hope, therefore, that I have evaded such charges by setting myself the strictly limited aim of producing a mere compass to lead the steps of the reader to the reliable guides listed in the *Select Bibliography* on page 192 of this book.

One major problem: in spite of more than a century of discussion, the transcription of Egyptian proper names into European forms seems no nearer universal acceptance, and in these circumstances, I have rendered royal and divine names by Greek versions, where these exist (thus *Sesostris* for Senwosret, Senusert, etc., and *Phiops* for Pepy or Pepi). I have renounced, too, the use of all diacritical marks favoured by Orientalists when writing among themselves. Wont and usage have also induced me to employ the somewhat imprecise geological terms favoured by the older Egyptologists (thus *granite* for porphyritic diorite, *green basalt* for arkose, and *alabaster* for calcite). The subject of chronology is still a thorny one, despite much recent research, and the system advocated by Professor Richard A. Parker has been fairly closely followed even when it is possible to differ from him in certain unimportant details.

Lastly I am greatly indebted to my Egyptological colleagues on both sides of the Atlantic for their prompt and cordial help in supplying photographs and illustrations and allowing me to publish them. In this respect my debt is greater than would appear from the brief acknowledgement under *Sources of Illustrations*. In particular, I owe special thanks to Mr George W. Allan, late of Cairo, who put his unrivalled collection of photographs at my disposal.

C. A.

CHAPTER I

The Discovery of Ancient Egypt

IT IS NOT PERHAPS surprising that the first Egyptologists should have been the Ancient Egyptians themselves. If a reverence for their past is evident at most periods of their long history it is what one might expect of a people with an almost bureaucratic respect for the sanctity of precedent. When King Nefer-hotep I (*c.* 1750 B.C.), for instance, decided to fashion a new statue of Osiris, the god of the dead, he searched among ancient archives in a library at Heliopolis for a pristine representation of the god so that its image could be made in proper and accurate form. Six hundred years later, Ramesses IV showed similar antiquarian leanings, and there are many instances where the works of a famous king have been meticulously copied by his successors.

Plate 63

But it was not only the Pharaoh, anxious to show he was heir of all the dynasties, who displayed such a vested interest in the past. By the New Kingdom at least, it was clear that a number of ancient buildings were regarded almost as national monuments and regularly visited by sightseers. When Queen Hatshepsut (*c.* 1480 B.C.) built her great mortuary temple at Deir el-Bahri and encroached on the precincts of the much earlier tomb of Queen Neferu, she was careful to leave a narrow tunnel so that visitors could gain access to Neferu's famous chapel; and the scribbles that these tourists have left on the walls suggest that they differed little from their modern counterparts. Such graffiti are also found in other monuments. One of several in the buildings around the Step Pyramid, for instance, telling us in stereotyped phrases that the scribe Ahmose came to see the temple of King Djoser and found it as though 'heaven were within it with the sun rising', reveals that this monument was open to sightseers over a thousand years after

Plates 38, 39

Plate 34

Plate 6

its foundation. It was not only the imposing temples of the mighty that were the object of such antiquarian interest. The modest tomb-chapels of private persons at Thebes were accessible to the curious nine centuries after the death of their owners, when in Saite times there was a great resurgence of pride in the achievements of the past, and selected reliefs and paintings were squared up for careful copying. By a rare freak of chance a Saite version in bas-relief has survived, as well as the original painting from which it was copied, and it is not a little reassuring to see that the extracts that appealed to the Saite artist are precisely those that have won our admiration.

Plates 52, 79

This study of his past by the Ancient Egyptian was often slip-shod, but a certain Ibi who made his tomb at Thebes during the reign of Psammetichos I (*c.* 600 B.C.) showed a remarkable thoroughness in copying scenes from a Dynasty VI tomb at Deir el-Gebrawi, over two hundred miles farther north, apparently because the owner had also been named Ibi and had borne a similar title.

c. 2250 B.C.

EARLY ACCOUNTS OF EGYPTIAN HISTORY

There must therefore have been a mass of records available to Manetho, the High Priest in the temple at Heliopolis, when he came to write in Greek his *History of Egypt* during the reign of Ptolemy II Philadelphus (*c.* 250 B.C.). This work has not survived intact but exists in fragmentary and garbled summaries preserved in the writings of Josephus and other Classical authors who quote from it merely to serve their own polemical ends. It is doubtful, however, even if a copy came to light whether it would be of more than limited value. Manetho's motive was only partly to inform an educated class of the story of his country. He wrote with particular bias, being involved in the rivalry of Ptolemy and Antiochus of Syria, each striving to claim a greater antiquity for the land he ruled. It is true that

Manetho would almost certainly have had recourse to all the archives that have survived today in a mutilated form, or to copies of them, such as the king-lists at Abydos and Karnak, preserving an Upper Egyptian tradition, and the lists of Saqqara and the Turin Papyrus giving a Lower Egyptian viewpoint. The Palermo Stone, which now exists in a number of scattered fragments, might then have preserved intact the annals of the earliest kings of Egypt up to the middle of Dynasty V. In addition, of course, Manetho would have had access to other and fuller documents which have not come down to us, and it is probable that his dynastic chronology would not have been wildly inaccurate. It is to be doubted, however, whether his interpretation of all the facts would have been equally impeccable since he had to rely on reports of events which, as we shall see, are suspect.

In default of Manetho's *History*, of special value is the account that the Greek traveller Herodotus (*fl.* 450 B.C.) gives in Book II of his *History*, where he deals with his tour of the Nile Valley. When he is reporting what he saw with his own eyes his opinions are generally shrewd and of considerable value; but much of what he recorded was mere hearsay, and he seems never to have come in contact with the educated classes of the country but was dependent for information upon local interpreters, guides, and petty officials, who like the dragomans of a later day were only too ready to pour a fanciful explanation into a credulous ear. He has thus preserved for us a number of contemporary folk-tales, often of great anthropo-logical interest but hardly of historical significance. Neverthe-less, it was upon the writing of Herodotus eked out by such other Classical geographers as Diodorus Siculus, Strabo, and Pliny that scholars had to rely until recent times for their picture of Ancient Egypt, since after A.D. 394 when the last-known hieroglyphic inscription was cut on the temple at Philae during the reign of Theodosius the Great, an impenetrable silence descended on the country in the face of its ancient past.

323 B.C.

The continuity of the native culture had indeed been broken centuries before when the Ptolemies succeeded to the Egyptian part of the Empire of Alexander the Great and sought to impose their alien Greek habits of thought upon its ruling caste. This Hellenization was ineffectual and by the time that the Romans annexed Egypt, in 30 B.C., Greek culture was but a thin veneer upon a predominantly native basis. Under the Romans, however, Egypt was ruthlessly exploited as a source of cheap grain for the city mob at Rome, and the exactions of successive prefects only provoked a nationalist spirit of resistance which found the Christian faith particularly congenial. This patriotic and religious movement, while it encouraged a revival of the Egyptian language in the form of Coptic, written in Greek characters and with Greek loan-words, led to no awakening of curiosity about the pagan past. Horapollo, it is true, writing in the later fifth century A.D. could show some mild interest in the now enigmatic inscriptions of his ancestors, but his attempts to explain the meaning of hieroglyphs were wide of the mark and only contrived to mislead future scholars.

The cleavage of Coptic Egypt from its ancient heritage was completed in A.D. 693 when Amr at the head of an Arab army captured the country for the Caliph Omar, and converted it to an Islamic State which severed for a millennium or more all intimate contacts with Christian Europe. The Moslems had no interest in Ancient Egypt except to eviscerate some of its standing monuments in the hope of unearthing the fabulous treasures they were thought to conceal. Otherwise, antiquities were regarded askance as the work of infidels, to be shown indifference or even the hostility of a certain Sheikh Mohammed who mutilated the Great Sphinx at Giza because he thought it would please God. The sympathetic study of Egypt's past had to await a fundamental change of mind; this came not from her own inhabitants, but from elsewhere.

The return in Western Europe at the end of the Middle Ages to the inspiration of its Classical past had a beginning in Italy where the tradition of humane learning had merely been overlaid. Here the ruins of a past grandeur were all around and inspired scholars to study their pagan ancestry: and not only the native past, but Antiquity itself. Some of the Egyptian monuments which had been carried off to Rome by the emperors were still standing; others imported to adorn the art galleries attached to Imperial baths and villas were brought to light during building operations throughout the sixteenth and subsequent centuries. The appearance in 1499 of Colonna's *Hypnerotomachia Poliphili*, an influential novel combining medieval symbolism with a new and imaginative antiquarianism, gives the first notable European example of an attempt to translate hieroglyphs according to an esoteric system that originates in the explanations of Horapollo. Up to the beginning of the nineteenth century, this belief that Egyptian picturewriting symbolically expressed abstruse religious and philosophical concepts was to persist. Nowhere is this theory more pronounced than in the writings of Athanasius Kircher (*fl. c.* A.D. 1650) whose reputation as a pioneer Coptic scholar is now a little tarnished by his fantastic interpretations of hieroglyphic inscriptions. For him the six signs that spell out a name of the Pharaoh Achoris (390–378 B.C.) meant that 'an accipitral statue with the feather and holy vase of the Nile is to be set up so that Momphta may be prevailed upon by prayer to grant the fertile increase of the Nile'.

Plate 29

The progress even of this feeble scholarship was woefully dependent upon the discovery of new antiquities and inscriptions, but only a thin trickle of these came into collectors' cabinets during the period, largely through acquisitions made by travellers, who in the age of the Grand Tour managed to broaden their minds, if not always their pockets, by a visit to the Near East. Thus the Rev. Richard Pococke, later Bishop of Meath, ascended the Nile as far as Philae in 1737, publishing an account of his voyage with engravings of antiquities he had seen or amassed *en route*. He, with other travellers such as Norden and Perry, and the antiquarian, William Stukeley, were members of the short-lived Egyptian Society, the first of its kind, formed in 1741 with the object of promoting Egyptian and other 'antient learning'. It was of such dilettanti that the satirical Addison made fun in his first number of *The Spectator* where he describes himself as making a voyage to Grand Cairo on purpose to take the measure of a pyramid.

A growing interest in Ancient Egypt throughout the eighteenth century was but one aspect of the developing Romantic movement which not only found the appeal of the past irresistible, but also was particularly attracted by a colourful Orientalism, a vivid *tourquerie*. It was not only to escape the hazards of Near Eastern exploration that Burckhardt travelled in native dress under the name of Sheikh Ibrahim. There comes into literature, and indeed all the other arts, a love for the picturesque Levant with its *bashi-bazouks* posing gracefully among ruins in a desert landscape. The inquiring traveller, complete with pencil and notebook, making his 'eothen' to ancient places, and his small audience of arm-chair scholars, with their groping speculations, were of course all thoroughly amateur, eclectic, and largely sterile; but they represent two distinct streams of activity which make up Egyptology even today.

THE BEGINNINGS OF EGYPTOLOGY

The dawn of a new era burst suddenly in 1798 when the French gave dramatic expression to an idea that they had cherished since the days of Colbert of seizing Egypt, digging a Suez Canal, and shortening the sea-route to India. It was left to Napoleon to attempt the realization of these dreams, but a true child of his time, he alone was responsible for a study of the Egyptian past in the process. His exhortation to his troops at the Battle of the Pyramids, 'Soldiers, forty centuries look down upon you', rings up the curtain on the Romantic discovery of Egypt. The baggage-train of his army included nearly two hundred savants whose business it was to explore, describe, and even to excavate. No such scientific expedition had till then visited any ancient site, and it set a pattern for several such missions in the new century. While Napoleon's adventure was militarily ill-fated, it firmly established French ascendancy in the cultural affairs of Egypt. The thirty-six illustrated volumes in which Vivant Denon and his collabora-tors described the monuments that they found in Egypt appeared between 1809 and 1813 and created the liveliest stir. Plate 1 From now on, the exploration of the past was to exercise the same fascination during the nineteenth century that the probing of outer space appears to have for our generation.

The results of the Egyptian expedition were far-reaching but not always to the benefit of scholarship. The operations of the French had been conducted as much for national prestige as for scientific gain. Egyptian antiquities now became pawns in a game of nationalistic rivalry which the various representatives of the then Great Powers played with each other, when the acquisition of a colossus of 'Memnon' or Plate 42 'Ozymandias' gave a nation the same delusion of grandeur as Plate 55 today would be achieved by putting a satellite into orbit. This competition began early in the century when by the Capitula-tions of Alexandria, the British seized possession of the Rosetta Stone, a large fragment of basalt inscribed with a text in Greek, demotic, and hieroglyphic scripts, which a French officer had unearthed while digging a trench at Rosetta in the Western Delta. Thereafter, the consuls of the various Powers and their agents vied with each other in amassing bigger and better *antikas*. It was this rivalry that filled the museums of the larger capitals of Europe with huge monuments which even today give the layman almost his only acquaintance with Egyptian Antiquity. During this period of 'unbridled pillage' almost as much was destroyed as was preserved. Tombs were opened with battering-rams or gunpowder; precious written records were reduced to disjointed scraps; hardly anything was secured with its pedigree intact. Into this spoiling of the Ancient Egyptians their descendants entered with as much zest as anyone, being only too eager to sell for Frankish gold chance finds that they neither understood nor cherished. In the process, antiquities were divided among several collectors, the head of a statue being acquired by one agent and the body by his rival. Papyri were cut up and the parts sold separately, thereafter to live apart for ever.

Plates 31, 70

Plates 58, 39

While adventurers of all sorts were reaping this rich harvest of antiquities and lining their pockets in the process, the scholars had not been idle. The discovery of the Rosetta Stone had at last provided a possible key to the centuries-old riddle of the hieroglyphs. While the stone was still in French hands Napoleon had had the inscriptions engraved and copies sent to the learned throughout Europe. The Greek text, which could of course be read and proved to be a decree in honour of Ptolemy V (196 B.C.), made it clear that the other two inscriptions in demotic script, the common language of the country, and in hieroglyphs, the monumental writing, were but versions of the same decree. Various scholars now took halting steps along the path of decipherment, the most notable perhaps being the English polymath Thomas Young who, applying the principles he had established from his study of the Rosetta Stone, was able to suggest that a certain group of signs in another bilingual inscription brought from Philae by the dilettante Bankes in 1819, spelled out the name of Cleopatra.

This discovery seems to have been notified to the French scholar Jean François Champollion and may have been instrumental in suddenly converting him from the then generally accepted view that hieroglyphs represented symbols not sounds. Unlike his rivals, Champollion was brilliantly fitted to exploit such a break-through. To his many natural gifts he added a knowledge of Coptic, and from his eventual recognition that hieroglyphs were merely a means of expressing in picture-signs a language which also survived in a greatly modified form written in Greek characters his progress was rapid. In 1822 his celebrated *Lettre à M. Dacier* first gave to the world a valid system for deciphering Egyptian hieroglyphs, and the phenomenal progress that his studies made in the short space of ten years before his early death, is seen in his *Précis* (1824) and in the grammar and materials for a dictionary that he left for posthumous publication. Almost at a blow the scientific study of the Ancient Egyptians had begun: for the first time since Theodosius they could speak through their own writings. The Statue of Memnon had become vocal again.

Champollion's successors carried the study of the ancient language to ever greater degrees of refinement so that today philology is a vast and separate study within the Egyptological ambit. The researches of Lepsius, Birch, Goodwin, Brugsch, Chabas, de Rougé, Maspero, Stern, Erman, and others in the nineteenth century, consolidated the ground won, and embraced also the intensive study of the hieratic and demotic scripts, as well as Coptic. In the present century the work of many philologists, but notably that of Möller, Griffith, Sethe, Gunn, and Gardiner, have resulted in an ability to read most Egyptian texts with a grammatical precision often keener than that of the ancient writer himself, even when the meaning is not entirely clear to our modern understanding. The greatest lack is in the documents themselves, the texts that have survived

Figs. 3, 9

being but a random sampling of the ancient literature. A free accession of new material, particularly of a literary, legal, scientific, or historical nature is badly required, not only to enlarge our understanding of the ancient past, but also to prevent the academic study of the Egyptian language from declining into a sort of Laputan parlour-game.

As the new knowledge of the language was disseminated among European scholars as a result of Champollion's discoveries, it became clear that yet another expedition was required to record more accurately the monuments of Egypt.

Plate 71

In 1828–9 Champollion himself, with Rosellini, the Italian Egyptologist, embarked on such a project, but the most notable of these undertakings was the Prussian expedition of Richard Lepsius, 1842–5. A vast store of inscriptional material from Egypt and the Sudan was published in 1859 in the twelve massive volumes of his *Denkmäler aus Aegypten*, consisting of plates only. The letter-press appeared posthumously in five volumes between 1897 and 1913. This still remains a funda- mental work and will hardly be entirely superseded as some of the monuments it records have since been destroyed or mutilated. Its accuracy, unhappily, is of a limited kind. The artists in the expedition worked with preconceived ideas and failed to reproduce the character of Egyptian drawing.

Precision and sympathy are found elsewhere, however, in the works of some other copyists, notably those of Robert Hay of Linplum (1799–1863), who in company with the artists Catherwood, Bonomi, and Arundale made several visits to Egypt before 1838 and there copied monuments and drew plans. Hay's invaluable manuscripts have, unfortunately, never been published except in extracts. Another amateur was John Gardner Wilkinson (1797–1875) who fell under the spell of Old Nile in 1821 and spent the next decade there copying and excavating. The results of his labours were largely embodied in his *Manners and Customs* (1837) with its quaint

Fig. 1   Orchestra and Dancers: woodcut after a drawing by Sir J. Gardner Wilkinson of part of a Theban tomb-painting now in the British Museum. See also p. 139

and appealing woodcuts. This work had a considerable influence in popularizing Egyptology among the educated classes
of Victorian Britain and is still not without its value. Later in
the century the work of recording surface monuments with a
progressive degree of accuracy became one of the most valuable
of the enterprises undertaken by the Egyptological societies
that were founded in Western Europe. In particular, the work
which Carter, Blackman, and Norman and Nina Davies
produced for the Egypt Exploration Fund (later Society) is
deserving of the highest praise and has set new standards of
attainment. The careful copying of monuments still goes on,
notably by the Oriental Institute of Chicago, and employs all
the resources of photography and other modern techniques for
securing and publishing a faithful record. Much, however,
still remains to be done in this particular field.

Plates 51, 52, 61
Figs. 14, 15, 39,
50, 51

Plates 59, 60
Figs. 22, 32, 41

At the middle of the last century Egypt was on the threshold
of a new era. The dynasty of the Albanian adventurer
Mohammed Ali seemed secure on its throne and the Court
and governing classes were becoming Westernized. Many
European doctors, engineers, bankers, merchants, missionaries,
and the like were assisting in the travail of Egypt as a modern

Power. The Suez Canal and the railways were about to make travel to Egypt, and within it, both swifter and safer. The admirable Mr Cook and Herr Baedeker were to bring the Nile Valley, already a sanatorium for wealthy invalids, within the reach of the middle classes of Europe. Egypt suddenly awoke to the fact that her monuments *in situ* were valuable tourist attractions. The old consular patrons and their minions had virtually disappeared, and the new men coming out to explore and dig were in search of knowledge not plunder, men like Howard Vyse (1784–1853) and Perring (1813–69) who surveyed the pyramids at Giza, Abu Rawash, Dahshur, and elsewhere; or Alexander Rhind (1833–63) who, like Wilkinson, first went to Egypt for his health's sake and stayed to study and investigate.

PROGRESS IN THE PAST HUNDRED YEARS

In 1854 an event occurred which was to have far-reaching effects on the rediscovery of the Egyptian past. A young French official of the Louvre, Auguste Mariette, was commissioned to go to Egypt and collect Coptic manuscripts, but while on a visit to Saqqara, thinking that he recognized half-buried in the sands monuments which seemed to mark an ancient site described by Strabo, coolly renounced his mission and 'almost furtively' began to dig. This enterprise which took him four years to complete, uncovered the vast Serapeum and greatly enriched the Louvre with antiquities of different periods. It also sealed his destiny, for in 1858 the Khedive Said appointed him Conservator of Monuments, and thereafter his life was dedicated to the excavation and preservation of the antiquities of Egypt on her own soil. The creation and development of an Antiquities Service to promote and regulate proper archaeological exploration and the establishing of a National Museum to display, conserve, and facilitate the study of

Egyptian antiquities, were the life-work of Mariette, who relentlessly carried out his mission in the face of obstacles from all sides—the intrigues of dealers and officials who were doing well out of the unregulated sale of *antikas*, the jealousies of other scholars who thought they could do better, and the indifference and treachery of the Khedive himself. The frustrations that Mariette suffered in his work would have broken the health and spirit of a lesser man; and in his energy and resilience, he may be said to have met fully the challenge of his time. Mariette's innovations were in the spheres of policy and administration. His methods are indistinguishable from those of his rivals: too much was attempted and his resources dissipated among too many sites, supervision was poor, inadequate field-notes were kept and very little was published. While Mariette's labours cannot be underestimated, much of what he achieved would have been lost if his immediate successor, another Frenchman, Gaston Maspero, had not succeeded him as Director-General in 1881. Maspero's long and diplomatic though interrupted tenure of office saw the firm consolidation of the shaky foundations of the Antiquities Service, the building of a worthy museum and the proper publishing of results. His learning, activity, and ability were all alike prodigious. He was the last of the giants, encompassing almost all departments of Egyptology within the grasp of his fertile mind, and bringing imagination and sympathy to his interpretation of the past.

Plates 9, 30, 33, 36, 38 54, 57, 82

By the eighties of the century, the exertions of such scholars and their popularizers had created a new patron for Egyptology —the educated middle classes of Europe and America who, banded together in learned societies, were prepared to give the financial support that hitherto had been provided only from wealthy individuals or State coffers. A lot of this good was done by stealth; and it was thought desirable to confront a public, brought up with a deep reverence for the Classics and the Bible, with aims they could readily grasp. Thus the prime object of the Egypt Exploration Fund formed in 1882, was to excavate in Egypt 'with a view to the further elucidation of the History and Arts of Ancient Egypt, and to the illustration of the Old Testament narrative . . . also to explore sites connected with early Greek History'. These latter objectives were faith-fully observed in the early expeditions of the Fund which in 1884 commissioned for their explorations at Tanis a compara-tively unknown surveyor, William Matthew Flinders Petrie (1853–1942), who was destined to revolutionize the technique of excavation in Egypt. Petrie was a man of no systematic education but with the most remarkable natural gifts which he dedicated entirely during his long life-time to the pursuit of Egyptian and Palestinian archaeology. Applying the principles of excavation, first invented in Britain by General Pitt-Rivers, and developing them in an Egyptian *milieu*, he broke entirely with the traditions of the old *déblayeurs* who were concerned only with uncovering substantial buildings from encroaching sands, or moving colossal monuments into museums. He paid attention to the many unconsidered trifles that had previously been overlooked or despised, the scribbles on potsherds, the broken bits of amulets and rings, fragments of crude domestic pottery, loose beads, discarded drill cores, all the dross and rubbish of Antiquity; and he showed that in their context they had a story to tell. Many of his innovations are now so much the accepted practice of field archaeology that it is difficult to believe that they were once revolutionary, such as the use of melted wax to secure fragile objects *in situ*; or the discovery of foundation deposits as a means of dating buildings and defining their limits even when they have been razed to the ground; or the study of the stylistic development and degeneration of artifacts as a means of dating, indeed the typology of such things as weapons, pottery, stone vessels, and beads owes a great deal to him. His main achievements in

Egyptology were his identification of the prehistoric cultures and his method of dating them by pottery sequences. He also more than anyone else uncovered the material remains of the early dynasties and brought them into some historical order, even on sites which had previously been rummaged by less skilful excavators. We cannot here list all the important monuments which were revealed and preserved in the course of his operations, but from a crowd of items we may arbitrarily select the palette of King Narmer, the ivory statuette of Kheops, the pectoral of Sit-Hathor-Yunet, the painted mud pavement *in situ* at Amarna which has since been spitefully destroyed, and the mummy portraits from the Faiyum. We might, however, have pointed to other achievements such as his finding the sites of Daphnae and Naukratis by tramping over the Delta mounds, or his early discoveries of Greek papyri in the ancient rubbish-tips of Hawara and Antinoe, in the Faiyum, opening up a rich field which others have exploited, or even the training of the Qufti workmen of Koptos during his operations there in 1894 to such effect that these men and their descendants have since served as skilled foremen on excavations all over the Near East. For half a century he followed the routine of excavating a site in the winter months and publishing the results in the following summer. His publications are an almost inexhaustible mine of information and are indispensable despite the faults occasioned by haste and often the exercise of a too imaginative leap to conclusions.

Plate 5
Plate 27

All this work was achieved on an extremely modest budget. He lived frugally on camp, often acting as his own photographer, chemist, copyist, artist, and handyman. Few of his collaborators could tolerate his now legendary standards of austerity. In his time he trained two generations of excavators, most of whom he outlived, and his methods were adopted and developed by others. Though he has had his critics, it will probably be found when the censure as well as the incense has cleared away that Petrie, like Mariette, was the man without whom Egyptology would be immeasurably poorer.

That is not to say, however, that little remains to be revealed by field archaeology in Egypt. The truth is rather that the surface of the subject has been little more than scratched. For expeditions depending upon private or public support some kind of spectacular result every season has been necessary in order to encourage the flow of funds; and scientific missions have therefore tended to concentrate upon the Upper Egyptian sites where the dry sands have preserved more of the past. The important but difficult Delta sites with their uncertain rewards have been generally neglected, despite the virtual disappearance in recent times of their ancient city-mounds under the mattock of the peasantry mining the *sebakh*, or nitrous soil of decayed cities, as fertilizer for their fields. More work of high quality is urgently needed at the unprepossessing prehistoric sites. The Early Dynastic deposits at Saqqara and Hierakonpolis equally demand systematic investigation. The thorough exploration of Tell el-Amarna awaits completion, the despoiled Royal reliefs of Dynasty IV may be buried in the ruined pyramid of Ammenemes I at Lisht, the foundations of all the buildings at Thebes require examination—but the list could be indefinitely extended. While with new building and irrigation schemes in Egypt the need for expert archaeologists has now become urgent, in recent years American and European expeditions have withdrawn their missions in the face of over-restrictive regulations. As these words are penned, however, the Egyptian authorities have announced plans for stimulating foreign participation in archaeological enterprises both in Egypt and Nubia; and it would seem that if their revised proposals are sincerely implemented, something of the old fruitful co-operation between the native Antiquities Service and foreign expeditions may well open a new phase in the work of preserving Egypt's heritage and elucidating its great past.

CHAPTER II

The Ancient Places

IN THE WEEKS OF July, the Blue Nile swollen with heavy rain changes into an immense mountain torrent, rising in spate and sweeping all before it. The raging flood grinds the boulders in its bed and carries the finer silt in suspension for thousands of miles. To this simple circumstance, Egypt owes her fertility, indeed her very existence and the character of her ancient civilization.

At the modern town of Khartoum, the Blue Nile is joined by the White Nile which flows from the vast natural reservoir of the great lakes of Central Africa and provides a steady flow of clear water throughout the summer months. Almost two hundred miles north of Khartoum the last great tributary, the Atbara, rising in the Abyssinian plateau, pours its flood into the Nile during the rainy season. At other times it shrinks into a number of pools within its sandy bed.

From this point northwards the great river flows in a vast sweep between leonine hills of Nubian sandstone. Its passage through this hot, fly-bitten region is impeded at five major points by reefs of harder igneous stone polished black by the action of the water and forming the cataracts or turbulent rapids amid craggy archipelagos. Between the Fourth and Third Cataracts stands Gebel Barkal, the southernmost boundary of Egypt at the time of its greatest expansion in the New Kingdom when the dependancy of Kush, as the Sudan territories were called, was under the charge of an Egyptian viceroy. From here, northwards, lie the sand-engulfed ruins of the outposts of Empire which the Egyptians built at this period at Sesebi, Soleb, and Amara.

At the island of Dal, the Nile enters the harsh and impressive hundred-mile-long gorge known as the Batn el-Hagar,

c. 1400 B.C.

or 'Belly of Stones', where it foams among the rocky islets of glistening granites, schists, and greenstone, which virtually form the Second Cataract. At its southern end lies Semna, the frontier of the Egyptian State during the Middle Kingdom, where the French archaeologist Jean Vercoutter has recently traced an early Nile dam built by Ammenemes III *c.* 1800 B.C. The ruins of the twin forts at Semna East and West crown rocky knolls in the vicinity, and from here northwards in the Batn may be traced the remains of six other fortresses founded mostly by Sesostris III to unite Upper Egypt and Lower Nubia into a powerful and easily defended province. These strongholds bear a close resemblance in character and purpose to the forts built by the British in North America during the Early Colonial period, being designed not only to control the savage and warlike tribes of the region, but to act also as trading-posts for the collection and dispatch of the local products: ivory, ebony, gold, hides, ostrich-feathers, gums, resins, and minerals. These forts, too, were really small townships in which the garrisons lived with their families. One of them at least was called after the reigning monarch, like any Fort William or George. With their massive walls of mud-brick, often more than thirty feet thick, strengthened with baulks of timber, their dry ditches, elaborate curtain-walls, fire-ports, loop-holes, barbicans, and drawbridges, they challenge comparison with any medieval Château Gaillard. Their most vulnerable point, the water-supply, was adequately secured by granite-roofed water-stairs to the near-by Nile. The garrisons kept in touch with each other by frequent dispatches in which movements in one area were duly reported to the neighbouring fortress. Despite these precautions, and the formidable defences, they were all stormed and destroyed, mostly by fire, during the anarchy that followed the collapse of the Middle Kingdom.

As the Nile leaves the Batn el-Hagar the monotonous inhospitality of the region is relieved by stretches of rich green

Plate 33

Plate 31
c. 1850 B.C.

c. 1680 B.C.

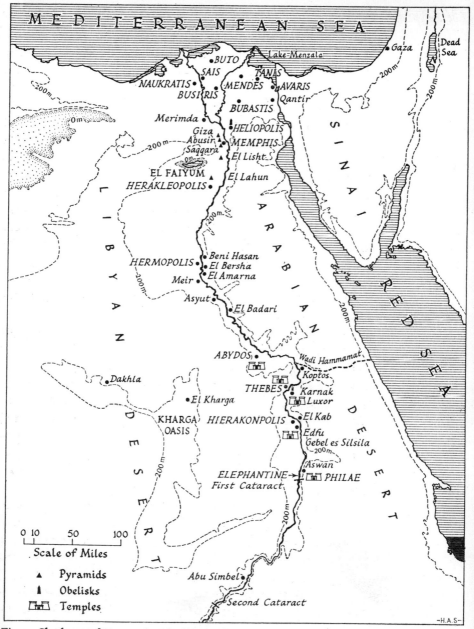

Fig. 2   Sketch-map of Egypt and Nubia showing the main sites. (Greek place-names are printed in capitals, modern Arabic locations in small letters.)

33

Fig. 3 Fragment of a dispatch written in hieratic on papyrus from a fortress near Abu Simbel reporting tracks of thirty-two men and three asses in the vicinity; c. 1839 B.C. Height 4½ in.

cultivation, especially where the cliff-like hills retire from the river-banks. Here, between the Second and First Cataracts, signs of Egyptian occupation in ancient times are increasingly evident. Opposite modern Wadi Halfa lies Buhen, the site of one of the most extensive of the fortress towns, the complete excavation of which is expected to yield dramatic results. Buhen marked the boundary of Kush and Wawat the ancient name for Lower Nubia. From here northwards, along the banks at different points stand the ruins of temples built by the Pharaohs of the New Kingdom, the most impressive of which are the two huge shrines hewn out of the living rock at Abu Simbel by Ramesses II. The colossi of the larger temple still smile at the sunrise between two opposite hills, as they have done for over three thousand years, unperturbed by their approaching death by drowning when the High Dam near Aswan is built. Numerous chapels, stelae, and inscriptions cut into the rocks mark the passage of various ancient viceroys and other officials on their way to and from their seats of government, and give imperfect echoes of the march of events in this region.

A little above Aswan the Nile leaves Lower Nubia and, forcing itself through a barrier of red granite hills which in its time it has reduced to a string of islands, enters Egypt near the old frontier at the First Cataract, a little above the island of Elephantine. There is no immediate change of scene: the river still flows in a chasm between tawny cliffs and the Nubian race, language, and culture extend almost as far as Gebel es-Silsila. At Edfu, however, nearly seventy miles farther north, the Nubian sandstone gives way to softer nummulitic limestone from which the Nile has scoured its ancient bed, and for the next three hundred and fifty miles the river flows between verges of rich alluvial soil hemmed in on both sides by arid desolation. On the west lies the Libyan desert, an immense eroded tableland broken by lines of shifting sand-hills and by

Plate 37

Plate 57

Plate 1

35

a string of fertile depressions which run almost parallel to the Nile. These oases are watered by subterranean wells supplied from the Nile water-table and their inhabitants have carried on a trade with Egypt in such products as aromatic woods, corn, fruits, hides, salt, natron, and minerals since earliest times. The Arabian desert on the east presents an awe-inspiring landscape as it thrusts a protective range of barren mountains rising to nearly seven thousand feet between the Nile Valley and the Red Sea. It is scored by deep *wadis,* or dry water-courses, which on occasions can become raging torrents as sudden and violent storms break out over the desert hills especially in winter. During such occurrences, rain-water may collect in natural cisterns, and a rich desert flora develops rapidly and carpets the stony ground for a season until scorched to extinction again. A number of springs, too, support a sparse vegetation and make a scanty subsistence possible for the flocks of the wandering Bedouin. Protected by these inhospitable deserts Egypt exists for most of its length as a narrow strip of cultivated land seldom more than seven miles in width and often much less.

At Edfu, the Nile flows past the ancient capital of the second *nome,* or district, of Upper Egypt where the temple of the sun-god Horus, built between 237 and 57 B.C., in the years of Egypt's twilight, is the most perfectly preserved monument of the Ancient World. A dozen miles north, at Kom el-Ahmar and el-Kab lie the ruins of Nekhen and Nekheb which together probably formed the capital of Upper Egypt in prehistoric times. The former site has been only sporadically dug, but has rendered up antiquities of the highest importance dating to the Late Prehistoric and Early Dynastic periods. Nekhen, the Hierakonpolis of the Greeks, had a hawk-god as its local deity, whereas the city goddess of Nekheb was the vulture Nekhebet who came to be regarded as the presiding genius of the whole of Upper Egypt and is frequently

Plates 82, 7

Plate 5
Fig. 45

associated with her counterpart, the cobra-goddess Edjo of
Buto and Lower Egypt, in heraldic devices.

Plate 54

From el-Kab the Nile describes a huge S-bend as far as
Koptos about a hundred and twenty miles farther north, and
almost mid-way between these two points on the east bank
stands the modern town of Luxor which with the adjoining
village of Karnak and other localities forms the site of Thebes,
the Southern capital at the period of Egypt's greatest development during the New Kingdom. It is from the many cemeteries
and ruined temples here that the bulk of the antiquities have
come which grace the collections of Europe and America; and
so many documents from this same source have contributed
to our view of the Egyptian past that we are now in danger of
interpreting Egyptian history with a distinctly Theban bias.

Plates 38, 56
Fig. 37

At Thebes the flanking hills on each bank retire to leave a
wide belt of cultivation and even the sober Baedeker is moved
to a lyrical appreciation of the scene: 'The verdant crops and
palms which everywhere cheer the traveller as soon as he has
quitted the desert, the splendid hues that tinge the Valley
every morning and evening, the brilliant, unclouded sunshine
that bathes every object even in the winter season, lend to the
site of Ancient Thebes the appearance of a wonderland, richly
endowed with the gifts of never-failing fertility.' Perhaps it was
something of this same feeling that moved an ancient poet
under Ramesses II to write a series of poems in praise of the
city and its god Amun, though he gets carried away by his
theme and makes the unsupportable claim that it is the most
ancient city in the world. Thebes rose to prominence only in
the Middle Kingdom when its local princes fought their way
to supreme power and ruled as Pharaohs over a reunited
Egypt. Throughout its history Thebes remained a centre of
resistance to alien rule from the north and after the expulsion
of the Hyksos by its princes, it won enormous prestige and
wealth as the main seat of government. It was here that the

c. 1250 B.C.
Plate 70

c. 2050 B.C.

c. 1570 B.C.

Pharaoh now had his tomb hewn in the rock of a lonely *wadi* on the west bank, the Valley of the Tombs of the Kings, while his mortuary temple stood apart from it in the plain below. Only one such sepulchre, that of Tut⁄ankh⁄amun, has been found substantially intact, the rest were pillaged several times in Antiquity and their royal occupants hurried from one hiding⁄place to the next until most of them had found a more lasting though undignified repose in two crowded mass⁄ burials. Their courtiers, who honeycombed the near⁄by hills with their tombs, fared no better, but the painted walls of their mortuary chapels have bequeathed us some memorial of their names and many lively scenes of contemporary life and aspirations.

The rise of Thebes naturally increased the influence and wealth of Amun whose great temple at Karnak became a sort of national shrine to which kings of all subsequent periods added their chapels and endowments. The brief but momen⁄ tous reign of the so⁄called heretic Pharaoh Akhenaten towards the end of Dynasty XVIII, when he moved the State⁄capital to Amarna, dealt Thebes and its god a shrewd blow from which it recovered in time though it was never again quite the same. Thereafter, it ceased to be the Pharaoh's Residence City though the tradition that he should be buried there after death continued to be observed until the close of the New Kingdom. Instead, Thebes gradually became the holy city of Amun, the king of the gods, who exercised his influence over the region at first through a High Priest and later through a human Consort, the daughter of the Pharaoh, and her Steward. Its sunset was long and blood⁄red. In the seventh century, it was sacked by the Assyrians. The Persians under Cambyses assailed it a century and a half later. Under the Ptolemies, the rival centre of Ptolemais eclipsed it in power and privilege, though it recovered some self⁄esteem for a time during the rebellion against Ptolemy V. It again revolted under Ptolemy X,

Plate 56

Plates 51, 52, 61
Figs. 14, 15, 46,
47, 51

c. 1370 B.C.

Plates 46, 43

Plates 67, 75, 74

38

and was recaptured after a lengthy siege which wrought great damage. Undeterred by its unlucky fate, it opposed the oppressive rule of the Romans in 30 B.C. and was thoroughly devastated for its pains. Of the 'hundred gated Thebes' mentioned by Homer, only a dozen damaged pylons among the temple ruins now remain.

Some hundred miles north of Thebes as the Nile flows, lies Abydos, the next ancient site of importance, near the modern village of el-Araba. Abydos was of very ancient foundation, the royal families of Dynasty I and their retainers building *c.* 3000 B.C. their tombs or cenotaphs here. The local god was originally a black dog-like creature known as 'Chief of the Dwellers in the West' (i.e. the realms of the dead); but by the end of the Old Kingdom, he had been assimilated by another and supreme death-god Osiris, probably in origin a deified pre-historic chieftain whose worship spread from the Delta city of Busiris to several sites in Egypt. Abydos rapidly rose to fame as his principal cult-centre, having the honour of housing in a reliquary the head of his dismembered corpse. The Egyptian antiquarians of Dynasty XVIII seeking here for tangible *c.* 1380 B.C. proofs of the ancient myth, mistook the cenotaph of King Djer of Dynasty I for the tomb of the god and so directed to it thereafter the votive offerings of generation after generation of pious pilgrims. This pilgrimage to the holy city of Abydos became an essential funerary ceremony and those who could not make their tombs near the burial-place of Osiris, had their mummies taken there by boat before entombment and participated in the water festivals that formed part of the Osirian mysteries; or made the journey by proxy. Other devotees Plate 22 contented themselves with setting up memorial tablets or statuettes in the precincts of the temple of Osiris, thereby assisting in the rituals or religious dramas. Besides such private monuments, cenotaphs were erected at Abydos by several kings throughout historic times. The most celebrated is the one built by Sethos I as a subterranean complex within a natural knoll representing the primal tree-girt mound of the cult. Associated with it was a magnificent funerary temple built of fine hard limestone which has allowed the sculptors of the reliefs full scope for delicate and detailed work of great technical brilliance. Its very perfection, however, tends to give an impression of little more than splendid nullity to the subject-

Plate 54

matter of the reliefs which are concerned entirely with repetitive religious ceremonies. Sethos I, one of the most pious kings who sat on the throne of Egypt, encouraged a restoration of ancient beliefs after the collapse of Akhenaten's religious innovations, and evidently associated with the god Osiris in this temple a number of deified ancestors from Menes the first Pharaoh onwards. Not the least valuable feature of these reliefs is the famous Abydos list of seventy-six predecessors whom Sethos considered important or legitimate enough to commemorate. So interested was he in this great enterprise that he built a palace at Abydos, whence he could follow the progress of the work.

There could be no greater contrast to this stronghold of orthodoxy than the next great site some hundred miles down-

Plate 43

stream, the modern Tell el-Amarna, the ancient capital of heresy. At this point the flanking cliffs on the eastern bank recede to leave a great semicircle about eight miles long. It was in this amphitheatre that one of the most fascinating dramas of the Ancient World was played out when the young Pharaoh Akhenaten was inspired to choose this spot as the site of his 'Horizon of the Aten', a Residence City dedicated to his new and sole god the Aten. Fourteen great stelae hewn on the rocks in the vicinity still demarcate the boundaries, and the half-finished tombs in the eastern cliffs, and the empty royal tomb in the side valley, still give some dim reflection of a light that failed. It is from their damaged reliefs and inscrip-tions that so many of our impressions have been formed of

Fig. 4   King Akhenaten, Queen Nefertiti and three of their daughters presenting elaborate perfume-holders to the Aten in the form of a sun-disk with rays ending in human hands: from a relief in the tomb of Apy at Amarna; c. 1362 B.C. Scale, 1 : 15

events during this distant time of crisis and experiment, of the family life of the King, the public investitures, the reception of foreign embassies, the lavish offerings to the Aten and the hymns and liturgy of the new faith. But the buried evidence has been no less vocal. Amarna is an archaeologist's paradise. Here on virgin soil a vast capital was run up, lived in, and abandoned all within two decades. So much has the past survived at Amarna that the track, for instance, that Penhasi, the Chief Servitor of the Aten, made by his daily walk between his house and the temple may still be seen on the desert surface in the evening light.

First Petrie, then the Germans, and then the British again

Figs. 39, 49

c. 1360 B.C.

have dug over the site and laid a great part of it bare. In the process much has been learned of town-planning and domestic architecture in Ancient Egypt. It is at Amarna that two of the most spectacular finds have been made in a land of sensational discoveries. One was by the German expedition of 1911–12, who found in the ruins of a sculptor's studio a number of statues, plaster casts, and portrait heads, including the famous bust of a queen, which have given us a new insight into the scope of Egyptian art and its techniques. The second and earlier discovery was made in 1888 when an old woman

Plate 45

Fig. 5   Cuneiform letter in the Metropolitan Museum, New York, from King Ashur-uballit I of Assyria to the Pharaoh requesting that diplomatic relations be established, and announcing the dispatch of a chariot and horses as a gift; c. 1350 B.C. Height $3\frac{1}{16}$ in.

digging for *sebakh* lighted upon the abandoned archives of the Foreign Office in the form of some three hundred clay tablets written mostly in Akkadian cuneiform, the international diplomatic language of the day. These tablets, which during their passage from one dealer's hands to another's suffered loss, damage, and destruction, proved to be copies of correspondence which had passed between the Egyptian Court and the royal households in Assyria, Babylonia, Anatolia, and Cyprus. The greater proportion of the tablets, however, is concerned with relations between the Pharaoh and the vassal city-states of Palestine and Syria. A most vivid and scarce-suspected picture has since emerged from the study of these sadly damaged lumps of clay. We see that in the literate world of the second millennium B.C. privileged officials, part-couriers, part-legates, and part-ambassadors, travelled from one Court to another bearing dispatches by which marriage treaties were arranged, trade-goods exchanged, extradition requested, diplo- matic alliances negotiated, protests submitted, demands made, aid requested, warnings administered, in fact all the features of a sophisticated system of international relations, with its own protocol, which differs little in essence from that of Europe in modern times and suggests an already long development before we catch this fleeting glimpse of it in action.

In the hills around Amarna are many ancient limestone quarries, the most renowned being the alabaster, more correctly calcite, quarries of Hat-nub, the 'Golden Quarry' as the Egyptians called it. Here numerous inscriptions scratched or scribbled on the walls by generations of stone-masons from the time of the Old Kingdom onwards, have furnished valuable evidence as to the unfolding of history in the larger Egypt beyond the galleries and abandoned workings.

Opposite Amarna on the west bank is the site of Khnumu, the ancient Hermopolis, cult-centre of the Ibis-headed Thoth, the god of writing and learning whom the Greeks equated with Hermes. Ramesses II erected a temple here largely built of stone pillaged from Amarna and recently excavated by the Germans. Its ancestry is, however, more venerable and in the Middle Kingdom it was the capital city of the 'Hare' district whose powerful princes were buried in the rock-tombs at Deir el-Bersha across the river. A statue of one of them has been found as far afield as Megiddo in Syria. In following the Nile northwards from here we shall also travel farther back in time as the predominantly New Kingdom sites of Upper Egypt give way to the Middle and Old Kingdom centres of Lower Egypt. The region around Hermopolis was full of thriving provincial towns during the First Intermediate Period and Early Middle Kingdom until Sesostris III put an end to the pretensions of the local feudal lords. At Deir Rifa, Asyut,

c. 1890 B.C.

Plate 31

43

Fig. 6 The ruined pyramid of Sesostris II at Lahun, from the south. The central rock-core consists of a natural outcrop on which originally a mud-brick superstructure about 160 ft high had been raised and held in position by stone walls and an outer limestone casing, later plundered by Ramesses II. Under the rubbish-mounds seen at the foot were discovered the entrance to the pyramid and the tomb of the King's daughter, Sit-Hathor-Yunet (see Plate 27); c. 1880 B.C.

and Meir southwards and Beni-Hasan northwards are important rock-tombs and cemeteries of the period which have contributed greatly to our knowledge of Middle Kingdom culture and politics. But a district closely associated with this particular period of Egyptian history lies farther downstream at the Faiyum depression which is really the most easterly of the oases in the Libyan table-land and lies only a few miles west of the Nile. The Faiyum with its lake, the Birket Qarun, is fed by a canal of ancient origin which enters the depression through a gap in the chain of Libyan hills at el-Lahun and waters the whole region. The Faiyum has been noted from early days for its wonderful fertility and pleasant climate, its vines, olives, wheat, and legumes. The earliest prehistoric settlements in Egypt have been found here. The vigorous kings of Dynasty XII increased its prosperity by improving its irrigation

Plate 35

c. 5000 B.C.

c. 1990–1790 B.C.

44

and built their residences in the vicinity at el-Lisht on the frontier between Upper and Lower Egypt. Here at el-Lahun, Dahshur, and Hawara on the desert margins they erected their stone and rubble pyramids which have ill resisted the hand of time and the despoiler. Nevertheless, treasures belonging to the royal ladies of the dynasty have been recovered from these sites and have bequeathed us a most impressive testimony of the fine taste and superb technical skill of the ancient Court jewellers. The Faiyum enjoyed a second period of prosperity during Ptolemaic and Roman times, and its rubbish-mounds and cemeteries have surrendered a great hoard of classical texts of all kinds written on papyri, which during the present century has revolutionized Classical studies—but that is another and different story.

Plate 27

Fig. 7   Granite-lined burial chamber in the pyramid of Sesostris II with the King's empty red granite sarcophagus, 9 ft long, hewn to an accuracy of one two-hundredth of an inch to the foot

45

c. 2600 B.C.

Plates 15, 18

Plates 10, 11, 13, 14

c. 2580 B.C.

Plate 24

These ruined Middle Kingdom pyramids form the southern-most end of a chain of such monuments that lie on the west bank of the Nile and mark the sites of the ancient Residence Cities of the Old Kingdom all the way to Cairo and north of it as far as Abu Rawash. At Maidum, to the south of Dahshur, and at Dahshur itself, there are some of the earliest pyramids still standing near the crumbling ruins of those of Dynasty XII. Clustered around each pyramid are the mastaba-tombs of the courtiers and officials of the day. The stone walls of the chapels or offering-chambers were invariably sculptured in low relief and painted with scenes which are the chief source for our knowledge of everyday life and funerary ritual and belief during the Pyramid Age. In a *serdab* or separate chamber, usually sealed off but connected by a spy-hole to the chapel, were stored statues of the owner and his family in painted wood or limestone, rarely in granite. Some of these tombs in their sculpture and statuary have preserved the artistic masterpieces of their day though hardly one is now in its pristine condition. The majority of these mastabas lie buried in the sands at Saqqara, where kings of Dynasties III, V, and VI built their funerary monuments, but others are at Dahshur, and yet others are at Giza near the most celebrated of all ancient tombs, the three stone-built pyramids of Kheops, Khephren, and Mykerinus of Dynasty IV.

These various cemeteries were near the Northern capital of Memphis of which scarcely any other record survives. Memphis was the premier city of Egypt, a vast metropolis, the 'white walls' of which were traditionally raised by Menes the first Pharaoh on reclaimed ground at the junction of Upper and Lower Egypt. It was a great religious and administrative capital throughout its long history. As a trading-centre all manner of crafts were carried on there, from ship-building to metal-work, under the auspices of the city god, the artificer Ptah, whose High Priest proudly bore the title of 'Greatest of Craftsmen'.

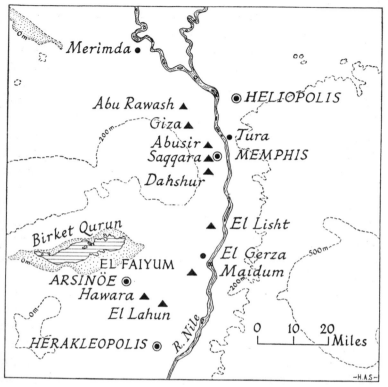

Fig. 8 *Sketch-map of the main pyramid sites of the Old and Middle Kingdoms*

Even in Roman times it was still prosperous and only suffered decline and extinction when the Arab conquerors pillaged its stone for building Cairo ten miles to the north on the opposite bank of the Nile. The modern village of Mit Rahina is the site of the temple of Ptah and near its palm groves the colossal statues which Ramesses II raised there have lain for centuries in fallen grandeur, though the smaller red granite specimen has recently been re-erected outside the railway station in Cairo as a monument to the new Egypt. Votive statues and other monuments from the temple site have come to light as a result

Plate 49

47

Fig. 9 Jar-fragment with hieratic docket in the Metropolitan Museum, New York, mentioning the contents and dated to regnal year 38 of Amenophis III; from the ruins of his palace at Thebes; c. 1360 B.C. Height 9¾ in.

of sporadic digging but the greater part of Memphis lies under the Nile silt and has not been systematically explored. Until this capital city is properly excavated our knowledge of Ancient Egypt cannot but be lop-sided.

A few miles below Memphis in ancient times the Nile divided into several branches as it wandered across the broad alluvium of its Delta, eventually entering the sea through seven principal and five secondary mouths. The region has always been one of great fertility and in Antiquity was flanked on its eastern and western borders by wide meadowlands where goats, sheep, and cattle were raised. The rich pastures produced both milk and honey and it was thither that the magnates sent their beasts to be fattened. Along the 'Western River', presumably the Canopic branch of the Nile, lay the large estates from which the Pharaohs obtained their choicest wines. Wine-labels in the form of dockets written in ink upon the jars themselves defined the particular *clos*, the vintage year, the name of the vintner, and the quality of the wine, suggesting that the Pharaohs or their butlers enjoyed a cultivated palate. In this rich plain among the water-courses stood the famous towns of Lower Egypt, Heliopolis, Bubastis, Sais, Buto, Mendes, and Tanis.

Heliopolis, the On of the Bible, was the centre of the sun-cult. Its temple was the largest in Egypt outside Thebes, and its high priests were the traditional wise men of Egypt, even in the Late Period when both intellectualism and the solar faith were in eclipse. The cult-object was the *ben-ben*, a stone

Fig. 30

of pyramid shape, usually elevated on a tall podium to form an obelisk, and one such monument erected by Sesostris I still stands among the fields in splendid isolation to mark the site of the great temple. The pair raised here by a later king, Tuthmosis III, now adorn London and New York under the incongruous name of Cleopatra's Needles.

Farther north lie the ruins of Bubastis, the Pi-beseth of Ezekiel, a city with an ancient foundation that goes back at least to the reign of Kheops and may well be earlier. It won some brief glory under the kings of Dynasty XXII who made it their Residence, enlarging the ancient tree-girt temple where the joyous festivals in honour of its city goddess were held. These pilgrimages by boat with fluting and castanet-playing were well described by Herodotus who was also impressed by the quantity of wine consumed during these feasts.

To the north-east of Bubastis, near the shores of Lake Manzala, are the ruins of Tanis, the Biblical Zoan, which has been explored by Mariette, Petrie, and most recently by the French Egyptologist, Pierre Montet. Scattered architraves, columns, and statue-fragments still mark the site of the temple which was largely built by Ramesses II and furnished with monuments usurped from his predecessors and hauled thither from other temples in the Delta. Tanis was once a prosperous *entrepôt* for the Levantine trade during the Late New Kingdom and grew to importance as the main seat of government during Dynasty XXI. Just before the war Montet made a brilliant discovery within the temple precincts of a group of tombs containing the remains of six kings of this period and their relatives. All the burials had been violated at one time and rearranged, but despite certain depredations, Montet was able to recover an extremely rich funerary equipment containing much gold- and silver-work and throwing new light upon the art, beliefs, and resources of an age which was contemporary with that of Solomon in all his glory. Tanis was not far from

c. 1950 B.C.

c. 1450 B.C.

c. 940–730 B.C.

Plate 30

Plate 69

c. 1000 B.C.

the great fortress of Tjel, the last outpost on the north-eastern frontier, and was always subject to influences from Asia. Somewhere near here was the site of Avaris, the armed camp built by the Hyksos to overawe their Egyptian subjects, according to Manetho; and there are scholars who identify it with Tanis. Also in the vicinity, perhaps at Qantir, was Pi-Ramesse the great treasure-city and Residence Town

c. 1304 B.C.

founded by the kings of Dynasty XIX and which a poet of the day describes as 'beauteous with balconies and dazzling halls of lapis lazuli and turquoise, the place where the chariotry is marshalled and the infantry assembles and where the warships come to anchorage when tribute is brought'. The crumbling mud-brick ruins of houses and a palace at Qantir are all that are left of this glory with the exception perhaps of a great

Plates 64-6

number of blue and polychrome faience tiles dispersed among different collections and which are doubtless the (artificial) lapis lazuli and turquoise referred to by the poet.

c. 664-525 B.C.

Of Sais, the wealthy Residence of the powerful kings of Dynasty XXVI, only 'inconsiderable' ruins exist near the modern Sa el-Hagar. Herodotus visited it soon after its apogee and describes the remarkable temple of the presiding goddess Neith, with its gigantic monolithic shrines and obelisks and its sacred lakes. He speaks too of the tombs of the kings in chapels of the temples, evidently similar to the earlier royal sepulchres at Tanis. Of all this nothing now remains.

Buto, too, the prehistoric capital of Lower Egypt, survives only as a few mounds near Tell el-Farain fifteen miles to the north; but in Herodotus' day it was a flourishing city with a noted oracle in the temple of Edjo, the cobra-goddess of the city and the presiding genius of Lower Egypt. From the top of the temple pylon it would have been possible to look over the flats and glimpse to the north what our Egyptian guide would have called the Great Green, and which we today call the Mediterranean.

CHAPTER III

The Natural Resources

WITHIN THESE BOUNDARIES Ancient Egypt disposed of many resources. When the inundation of the
Nile was neither too profuse nor too scanty, the tremendous
fertility of the soil brought forth crops of all kinds, wheat and
barley, figs, grapes and dates, melons, cucumbers, onions,
leeks, lettuces, radishes, peas, and beans. Wine was pressed
from grapes and also fermented from dates and from palm-sap.
Beer, similar to the modern Nubian *bouza*, was brewed daily
in the larger households. Vegetable oils used in cooking,
lighting, cosmetics, and medicines were chiefly derived from
the fruits of the balanos and moringa trees and from the castor-
oil plant. The olive was introduced comparatively late and
never became an important source of oil. The papyrus plant
abounded in the Delta and the undrained areas of Upper
Egypt and supplied a host of needs from food prepared from
the rhizome to cordage made from the stalks. Linen in all
grades, from a very fine quality for the best clothing, to very
coarse canvas, was woven from the fibres of the flax plant.
Baskets and matting were made from grasses and rushes and
the leaves of the *dom* and date-palm.

Egypt supported a large cattle population. The chief ceremonial meat offerings were usually of beef in the form of head,
legs, ribs, and offal. But herds of sheep, pigs, and goats were
also raised and while there is no reference to suggest that their
meat was ritually eaten, dockets from jars which contained
goat's fat have been found in the ruins of the palace of
Amenophis III at Thebes. Even if fabrics made from goat's
hair and sheep's wool have not been found until the Classical
period there is no doubt that certain garments, such as shawls,
were woven from these fibres from earliest times though they

Fig. 10   Butchers cutting up a sacrificial ox, from a relief in the tomb of Ti at Saqqara; c. 2380 B.C. Scale, 1 : 6

were evidently considered as ceremonially impure and not deposited in the earlier burials. Parchment, goat's skin, and other hides were, however, tanned and dyed for a multitude of purposes, from writing-materials and cushion-covers to harness and footwear.

Plate 26

Milk was an important farm-product and cheese and butter were prepared from it, though the evidence is scanty. The same flowery meadows that fattened the prize cattle so that their legs became bowed under the weight of their bodies, also produced honey which was used, as in Europe until recent times, as a main source of sugar. In addition, the pods of the carob or locust-bean tree were used for sweetening purposes.

Plate 16
Fig. 32

The Nile and its pools abounded in fish, and the lakes with water-fowl. Salt and natron were always to hand for preserving fish and meat, which could also be 'jerked' or sun-dried.

The Egyptian farmers in their early experimental phase tried to domesticate such animals as hyenas, gazelles, and cranes but gave up the hopeless struggle after the Old Kingdom. Flocks of geese were, however, raised from earliest times and supplied eggs, flesh, and fat: the domestic fowl does not make

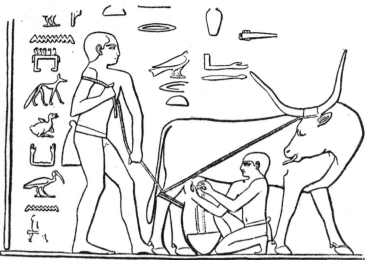

Fig. 11 Milking scene, from a relief in the tomb of Kagemni at Saqqara; c. 2330 B.C. Scale, 1 : 6

its appearance until Ramesside times and then only in isolated instances. Cats, gazelles, geese, monkeys, and dogs were bred as pets. Burials of dogs near the tombs of their masters have been found from the time of Dynasty I. Apart from a species of lap-dog, like a dachshund, there were *slughi* hounds for use in the hunt. Game, from lion, wild cattle, and asses, to oryx, ibex, hare, and ostrich were hunted or trapped on the verges of the cultivation. The hippopotamus was already sufficiently rare by historic times to have lost importance as a food animal but it was occasionally hunted for sport. The elephant had become extinct in Egypt during the Prehistoric Age, but its valuable tusks were imported from the Sudan where it still roved at large. The only beast of burden was the ass, though cows were used for ploughing. The horse did not appear until the end of the Middle Kingdom and was used almost exclusively for drawing a light chariot. Camels are not known before Classical times.

c. 3000 B.C.

Plate 59

Plate 28

Fig. 50
Plate 52
Fig. 39

Fig. 12   Fattening cranes with prepared food-pellets, from a relief in the tomb of Ti at Saqqara; c. 2380 B.C. Scale, 1 : 6

Only in one thing was Egypt notably lacking, and that was in good constructional timber which had to be imported from the Lebanon, a traffic which is probably as old as the sea-going ship. The native trees, mostly acacia and sycamore-fig, were too knotty and unresilient to provide good quality timbers though they were used for simple domestic furniture, boxes and coffins, and were often veneered with ivory, ebony, and other woods to make a better appearance. The Egyptian from earliest days was skilful in exploiting various rushes and reeds, in the making of all sorts of articles in wickerwork such as tables, stands, stools, and boxes. For building generally an excellent material was near to hand in the Nile mud which

Fig. 14

when mixed with straw develops great plasticity and may be moulded into bricks which are then sun-dried. This ancient technique is still practised today and modern excavators for instance have built expedition houses out of ancient bricks supplemented with modern ones made on the spot. The mortar and rendering were the same colloidal mixture of mud and straw. Such mud-brick buildings are cool in summer and warm in winter, and since Egypt is generally a rainless land, stand up well to the weather. Domestic building in Egypt from the simple hovel of the peasant to the lime-washed and painted palace of the Pharaoh was in the same mud-brick. The renewal of worn floors and walls was a simple matter.

Plate 43

The Egyptian, however, had almost from the start an urge to build the 'eternal dwellings' of his gods in more durable materials and for this, ample supplies of good building stone lay all around, from the limestones of Upper and Middle Egypt to the sandstones of Lower Nubia, both easily quarried into blocks along their planes of cleavage. But in addition, the Egyptian used hard and intractable stones—granites, basalts, and quartzites which were obtained often from remote regions such as the Wadi Hammamat and the Nubian deserts.

For most of its ancient history Egypt lived in the Bronze Age, or rather the copper age, bronze not coming into general use until the New Kingdom. Copper-ore was mined in Sinai and at sites in the Arabian desert and copper ingots were imported in later times from Syria and Cyprus. For most of

c. 1570 B.C.

Fig. 13 The hound 'Victor' under his master's chair, from a painting in the tomb of Weser, No. 21 at Thebes; c. 1480 B.C. Scale 1 : 10

Fig. 14 Servants of the Vizier Ramose carrying rush-work stands and wooden boxes in his funeral procession; from a painting in his tomb, No. 55 at Thebes; c. 1368 B.C. Scale, 1 : 10

her history, ample supplies of this vital metal were procurable within her own borders. The forging of iron, however, lagged behind the craft in other countries of the Near East. Egypt played no part in the early development of iron and laboured under a handicap in consequence in her later years. She had, however, immense gold-bearing regions lying in the Arabian desert, in Nubia, and in the Lower Sudan and these deposits were all thoroughly exploited in Antiquity. The gold occurred naturally alloyed with varying amounts of silver, from fine gold through electrum to white gold, regarded by the Egyptians as silver, a rarer material than yellow gold. The baser alloys of gold were used for hard soldering the purer grades. These desirable metals made Egypt wealthy in a world which

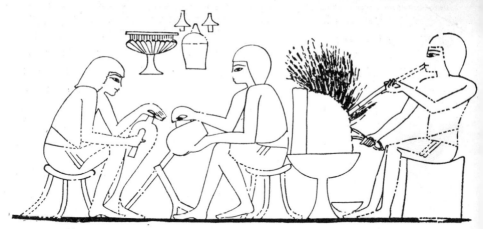

Fig 15 Goldsmiths chasing, raising and soldering metal vessels, from a painting in the tomb of two sculptors, No. 181 at Thebes; c. 1380 B.C. Scale, 1 : 4

recognized a kind of gold standard in international trade. To other nations of the Near East, it was proverbial that gold was as dust in the land in Egypt.

In all these natural resources, and in some of her native industries, such as weaving, paper-making, and fine joinery, Egypt was rich and powerful and well equipped to play a leading part in the world of her heyday. Well might the Israelites in the wilderness of Zin bewail the loss of the flesh-pots of Egypt which they had enjoyed even as a subject-people.

In tracing the course of the Nile through the lands of Egypt in modern times we cannot fail to remark a certain difference between the human inhabitants on the river-banks as we travel north. The Upper Egyptians are darker-skinned and of slighter build than their more sedentary neighbours in the North and speak a different dialect. This distinction was apparent even in ancient times when it was a maxim that a man of Elephantine would find himself at a complete loss in the Delta. The Upper Egyptian looking across his little world of the Nile cultivation could see the hostile desert hemming him in on both sides and knew that only his ceaseless toil kept the barren red sands at bay. The work of irrigating and extend‑ing the black fertile verges of the Nile was most successful when performed on a large scale, and in this the Upper Egyptian early learnt the virtue of co‑operating with his neighbours. The river flowing through the entire region in one broad flood assisted the process of cohesion by providing an easy means of communication with every part.

Lower Egypt, on the other hand, was a wide expanse of streams, creeks, and marshes isolating the larger pastures. Its Mediterranean climate was wetter and kinder than that of the arid South. The Nile which unified Upper Egypt, by dividing anciently into twelve major branches and innumerable rivulets parcelled Lower Egypt into a dozen or so individual principalities each with a large town at its centre of government. While Upper Egypt could only look northward to its richer neighbour, Lower Egypt faced its seaboard from whence peoples and ideas from the Eastern Mediterranean reached it. In early days it is presumed to have been culturally more developed than the rural South. In historic times, particularly during the Old Kingdom and Late Period, it maintained its lead as the centre of the arts and crafts, attracting skilled workers and learned scribes from near and far. It was, however, always at a disadvantage with its Southern neighbour, being by nature politically fissile.

This antithesis between Upper and Lower Egypt was recognized by the Egyptians themselves who saw their world as an essential equipoise between two opposites. This attitude may in fact have over‑accentuated the contrast, since while superficially so different the 'Two Lands' were fundamentally alike. They shared a common population, shading perhaps from a pure Hamite in the South to a more Mediterranean mixture in the North, but speaking a common language and having the same material culture and spiritual outlook.

The prehistoric Egyptians belonged to the Mediterranean race; they were a slight people with long heads and delicate oval faces. Their hair was dark and wavy but scanty upon their bodies. They are presumed to have spoken a Hamitic tongue akin to that of the Berbers of Libya or the Somalis of East Africa; originally hunters and cattle-raising nomads, they were obliged by circumstance to settle in the Nile Valley and cultivate the soil. This basic stock was modified at an early period by broad-headed migrants from Palestine of mixed Anatolian and Semitic descent to produce the historic Egyptians, glabrous, moderate in stature, with massive skulls and strong bones, the wrists and ankles being particularly thick. The women were generally shorter and more slender, and like the modern peasants whom they closely resemble, rarely became corpulent. The infiltration of Armenoid blood was fairly continuous from the North throughout historic times and tended to produce a racial type which varies from the heavy and muscular Northerner to the lean, sun-tanned, and lightly built Upper Egyptian.

Plate 14

The amalgam of Asiatic and African races in the ancient population is repeated in the language they spoke which is related to the Semitic tongues in much of its grammar and vocabulary but yet has affinities with Hamitic languages also, suggesting a fusion of two tongues in much the same way as Anglo-Saxon in England was modified by Norman French to produce English. The Egyptian language, however, had its own peculiarities, and if speech is but a natural expression of the genius of a people, we must remark that Egyptian is characterized by its conciseness, concrete realism, and keen observation. It has, as Gardiner points out, a preference for the static over dynamic expression and apart from some rare survivals has no genuine active tense. In other words, it has very much the character of its own picture-writing, where by acute observation the essential appearance of an object has been reduced to an unambiguous heraldic device with which it is impossible to render abstract ideas with any precision despite the continuous development it underwent in thousands of years.

The fundamental racial type of Ancient Egypt remained remarkably constant throughout historic times and is still apparent among the peasantry in the remoter areas of Upper Egypt, who where they have not been stultified by excessive toil and disease are remarkably ebullient and resourceful, undemanding and thriftless, quick-tempered but not resentful. Much of this disposition is also evident in the Ancient Egyptians as they have revealed themselves to us.

Herodotus regarded the inhabitants of Upper Egypt in his day as among the healthiest in the world and certainly the region with its sunshine and dry winter climate has always attracted invalids from the days of the Romans. But pathologists who have examined Egyptian mummies have claimed to identify some of the lesions of several ailments that trouble the modern fellahin, notably rheumatism and water-borne diseases. While the birth-rate was doubtless high, the infant mortality rate was far from low and it has been computed on somewhat insecure foundations that the population in Dynasty XI did not greatly exceed a million, though in a valley which still had vast undrained areas, this meant quite a concentration of human beings in scattered towns and villages.

While the Ancient Egyptians prayed for a good old age and set the ideal life-span at a hundred and ten years, the average expectation of life in Graeco-Roman times has been estimated at about thirty-six years and there is no reason to believe it was any higher in Pharaonic days. To offset this, in common with so many of the nations of Antiquity in the Mediterranean, the Egyptians matured early, puberty being attained at the age of twelve and official manhood at not more than sixteen. Heavy responsibilities were undertaken by people whom we should now regard as children. A certain nomarch of Asyut relates that the King appointed him governor of a province when he was only a cubit high and made him learn swimming with the Royal children. The High Priest of Amun, Bakenkhons, who entered the priesthood on reaching manhood, had already spent some years as Chief of the Training Stable of Sethos I. Three successive Pharaohs of Dynasty XVIII were ruling over their large territories before they had passed their twelfth, sixteenth, and ninth years respectively. Of course such statistics can be as misleading as any average, and the short and youthful reign of Tut-ankh-amun, for instance, can be offset by that of Phiops II who had the longest recorded reign in history. Nevertheless, there is sufficient evidence to show that much of the Egyptian achievement was secured by an extremely youthful population schooled by strong traditions rather than by personal experience.

CHAPTER IV
The Rise of Egypt

OUR KNOWLEDGE OF the course of events in Egypt has been derived from various sources. There are the disjointed reports of Herodotus, Manetho, and other Classical writers, less and less reliable the farther they penetrate into the past. The Old Testament has bequeathed us a few biased references to contemporary or near-contemporary events; and scanty accounts from other foreign sources also exist, such as the Hittite State records, and the archives of Assyria and Babylon.

The evidence from Egypt itself is of two kinds, the literary and the archaeological. There are firstly the written records in letters, autobiographies, lists of rulers, temple inscriptions, and the like. Although nearly all this material is greatly damaged and incomplete, some of it is of great value, such as the laconic statement of important achievements under each king on the fragmentary Palermo Stone, or the foreign correspondence from Amarna, though the proper sequence in which the letters should be put remains doubtful. But many of the official pronouncements which the Pharaohs left for posterity are no more than mere propaganda designed to sustain the god-like status of the ruler, and Egyptologists in the past have been a little naïve in accepting them all at their face value. It is doubtful whether the Egyptians had any idea of history as we know it and in the words of the late Stephen Glanville, 'it seems highly improbable that the most patient and prolonged study of their almost unlimited remains will ever enable us to do for them what they did not seek to do for themselves, and that is to write their history'.[1] We need not, however, entirely accept this counsel of despair since we can by archaeological

[1] S. R. K. Glanville: *The Growth and Nature of Egyptology*, p. 35.

investigation exert certain checks upon the official narrative, where it exists, trimming the outline here and there to a more plausible shape and in the process charting some of the mental workings of the ancient redactors. The discipline is similar to that employed by intelligence services in war-time to discover their opponents' plans and resources. In this work of detection every scrap of information must be fitted into a complicated mosaic; and deduction and circumstantial evidence have an important part to play. One may give as an example of this technique, Winlock's reconstruction of the order of the kings of Dynasties XVI and XVII from the itinerary taken by a Commission who visited the royal tombs of the dynasties some five hundred years after, and whose report has survived as the Abbott Papyrus. But it must be confessed that much of our evidence is woefully inconclusive even when it is tangible. Thus we know from his actual mummy that King Seken-en-re Tao II died of frightful wounds, but whether on the field of battle or at the hands of assassins is still disputed. The problem of finding out what happened in Ancient Egypt is truly formidable and is not lessened by the uneven wealth of the material remains which often tend to confuse the picture with intractable detail. Forty years ago, for instance, the Amarna period seemed a startling but clear-cut interlude in the Egyptian story. Today as a result of fresh evidence brought to light by excavations during the inter-war years, the outlines have become blurred, and scholarly opinions are vehemently opposed.

In this and the following four chapters we shall attempt to sketch in outline the cultural history of Egypt from its pre-historic beginnings to the death of the last native Pharaoh in 341 B.C. For this purpose we shall employ Manetho's time-honoured system of arranging the reigns of the various kings into thirty-one dynasties, which Egyptologists further group into the Old, Middle, and New Kingdoms and the

Late Period, each characterized by a homogeneous civilization and divided from each other by interludes of political confusion. The Egyptians dated events to the reign of a particular king from his first year of rule onwards, beginning again with each change of Pharaoh. The exact length of reign has, however, been recorded only in a few cases. For some periods it is even uncertain whether the full list of kings and their proper order of succession have survived. The chronology of Egypt has therefore had to be established by modern scholars largely by working backwards and forwards from one or two fixed points determined from chance records of astronomical phenomena. Thus the heliacal rising of the star Sirius recorded in year 7 of Sesostris III can be calculated to have occurred in 1872 B.C. Despite much recent research there are still margins of error particularly for the earlier periods of Egyptian history. The prehistoric ages have been identified purely by archaeological investigation at various sites in Upper and Lower Egypt, and their dating has recently been controlled by radio-carbon analyses.

I. THE PREHISTORIC AGES

During Late Palaeolithic times, the retreat of the ice-cap in Europe caused climatic changes in North Africa which gradually became drier. The Nile from being a vast inland lake had shrunk progressively towards its present bed leaving behind eight terraces flanking the hills of the Libyan and Arabian deserts, on the lower four of which the characteristic worked flints of the Early Stone Age have been picked up. In their search for water, the inhabitants of the region were steadily forced into a greater concentration on the verges of the Nile, and it was here that the gradual transition from a hunting to a food-producing economy must have occurred. These early settlers found a valley full of reedy swamps and shallows left by the Nile flood every year and teeming with fish and fowl besides hippopotamus and crocodile. Such conditions persisted to an ever-decreasing extent in historic times though they have since retreated to the Upper Sudan. The *wadis* that flanked the river with their meadows and low shrubs supported lion, ass, wild cattle, Barbary sheep, ibex, antelope, and other desert game hunted by generations of Egyptians throughout Prehistoric and Pharaonic times.

Plate 59

The first settlers must have found no great compulsion to change their nomadic way of life. Game, fish, and fowl could be hunted or trapped in the Valley, and edible roots such as the papyrus rhizome or plants like the wild Abyssinian banana could be gathered when ripe. But later migrants, presumably from Palestine, brought with them the novel craft of the husbandman, sowing barley or emmer wheat in ground left moist by river flood or rainstorms, and squatting in the vicinity while the crop was growing and being harvested. At some point in this shadowy past, a family or other group of these cultivators must have taken the decisive step of settling permanently in one place to grow these cereals as a main food. There was every incentive for them to do so. For abundant crops could be raised merely by scattering seed on ground ploughed, manured, and watered all in one process by the Nile inundation, and treading it in by foot or hoof. The grain germinated and ripened in the gentle heat of winter and spring. The production on a large scale of food crops that could be stored indefinitely, especially in the dry desert margins, was the first step in a revolution that was to replace a wandering, hand-to-mouth existence by an urban civilization based on agri-culture with all that that has meant to mankind in the storing of surplus food, the domestication of animals, the creation of leisure, the specialization in various arts and crafts, and the exercise of some conscious control over the future. In Egypt, particularly as the pressure of population increased, it led to attempts to harness the annual inundation of the Nile and to distribute it over ever-widening tracts of land. The Egyptians soon found that such work was most effective when it was done by co-operative effort on a large scale. The transformation of the destructiveness of the inundation into a power for good accustomed the Egyptians to an organized way of life and instinctively encouraged the development of local political and religious institutions to direct such undertakings and en-sure their success. The inevitable result of this process was the unification in historic times of the entire country under a single government as small families of settlers coalesced into village communities, and these in turn grouped themselves into the historic *nomes* or provinces as the exploitation of the land became more extensive.

2. EARLY PREHISTORIC PERIOD

Stages in the long journey of the Egyptians towards civilization have been recognized as a result of excavations at various sites. But even the outlines of this story are still very sketchy and the sequence of events highly conjectural. Two broad phases in the development can at present be traced. The first, or Early Pre-dynastic Period, covers much of the excavated material as found at the Neolithic sites of Deir Tasa in the South, and Faiyum 'A' and Merimda in the North, and extending through the Chalcolithic cultures of el-Badari and el-Amra, near Abydos, again in the South (see the chart opposite).

From a survey of the material remains in the first category we can see how the early Egyptians gradually adapted them-selves to an agricultural way of life which, by the end of the period about 3600 B.C., probably differed little from that followed by the pagan tribes of the Upper Nile today. At this point, we find both wheat and barley being grown and stored in pits lined with mats. Basketry was practised and the

Date B.C.	Northern or Lower Egypt	Southern or Upper Egypt	Main Sites	Period
c. 5000	Faiyum 'A'	Tasian	Faiyum depression Deir Tasa, Mosta-gedda	Neolithic
c. 4000	Merimda	Badarian	el-Badari Merimda	Chalcolithic
		Amratian	el-Amra, Nagada, el-Ballas, Hu, Abydos, Mahasna	Early Pre-dynastic
3600				

Table A Early Prehistoric Period

technique of weaving linen improved steadily throughout this period. Garments were also made of animal skins which could be tanned and softened. Needles were of bone. Bracelets of ivory and shell, and perforated stone and shell disk-beads are common. Eye-paint, ground from green malachite on schist palettes, and cleansing oils, expressed from the wild castor plant, show that the cosmetic arts, always important in the hot and dry Egyptian summer, were developing. Combs, made from bone or ivory, are decorated with figures of animals in Amratian times. Tools and weapons were almost exclusively of stone or flint, arrows being tipped with chert points as well as bone barbs. The throw-stick, probably used in fowling, was known in a form that differed little from that used in Pharaonic times. A mace with a pear-shaped stone head becomes common by the end of the Amratian period. During this phase food was apparently plentiful. Dogs, goats, sheep, cattle, geese, and pigs had been domesticated and wild game abounded. Grain was probably boiled for porridge as well as baked for bread. Cooking and storage vessels were of pottery and the ceramic arts show a steady advance from the coarse

Fig. 17

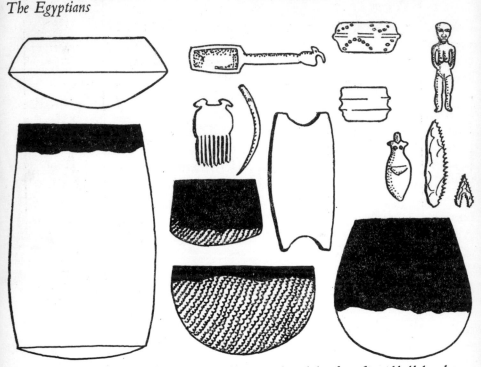

Fig. 16   Group of Badarian artifacts: black-topped pottery with combed surfaces; flint sickle-blade and arrow-head; slate palette; ivory scoop, bracelets, needle and comb; ivory and clay figurines of women; c. 4000 B.C.

clay cups and bowls of Faiyum 'A' to the fine, red, burnished pottery of the Amratians with its fanciful shapes and linear decoration in white slip. Vases hollowed out of stone also appear during this phase, the precursors of one of the most characteristic products of historic Egypt.

The spiritual life of these early inhabitants of the Nile Valley can never be known to us. They evidently believed in a hereafter for some members of the community, since in the burials of the period the body is usually crouched on its side as though awaiting rebirth and is accompanied by pots, weapons, cosmetic palettes, and sometimes rudimentary clay or bone figurines of women, which suggest that this after-life, for the male at least, was expected to make the same demands upon him as he had known on earth. Faint echoes of primitive beliefs which must date to these Prehistoric times can be caught in later Pharaonic religion. From them it has been surmised that the earliest Egyptians worshipped sky- and star-deities and that their leaders were doubtless rain-makers who, as in the Sudan recently, were ceremonially killed, perhaps by drowning or dismemberment, when their powers began to wane. The political system under which these people lived is equally obscure. Probably communities were small, self-supporting, and relatively isolated around village centres: but copper pins and glazed steatite beads in Badarian and Amratian deposits reveal that trade was carried on with more advanced cultures elsewhere.

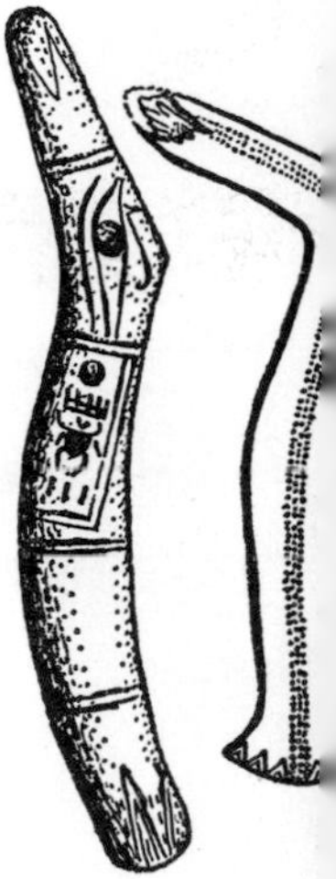

Fig. 17   Model throw-sticks; one in wood from Badari, c. 4000 B.C., the other in blue faience from the tomb of Tuthmosis IV; c. 1397 B.C. Scale, 1 : 5

3. LATER PREHISTORIC PERIOD

This essentially African culture might have remained barren at this stage of development, as it did in the Sudan for much longer, if it had not been fertilized by vigorous contacts from Asia whence some significant introductions now came. Copper tools and weapons, for instance, become more common, though flint continues to be used in Egypt for centuries in such processes as the grinding of stone vessels, the carving of ivory, and the reaping of grain. The introduction of the techniques of copper-working may have stimulated the Egyptians to gain control of Sinai and the Arabian desert where in historical times their main ore deposits were mined. But other influences from farther afield also appear during this later phase of the Prehistoric period. Such techniques as build-ing with rectangular sun-dried mud-bricks, imprinting clay

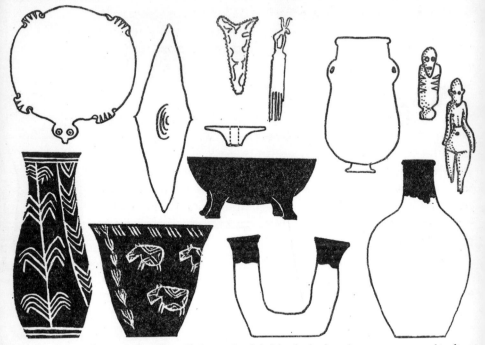

Fig. 18   Group of Amratian artifacts: black-topped polished bowls, bottle and two-spout vase; white linear designs on red pottery, one with figures of hippopotami; slate palettes, one in the shape of a tortoise; ivory comb; amulet carved from a tusk; bone figurine of a woman; flint lance-head; stone mace-head and footed vessel; c. 3600 B.C.

cf. *Fig. 38*   with cylinder-seals, the use of certain new styles of ornamenta-tion, and the first attempts at a pictographic system of writing have been traced by some scholars to a Mesopotamian source. While these innovations coincide with a drift of broad-headed peoples, perhaps originally from Anatolia or Syria, into the Southern regions to modify the long-headed Hamites, they have no appearance of being imposed by conquest. All the evidence is that this spread of foreign influence in the fourth millennium B.C., like that in the second, came from the North, but our picture of conditions in the Delta at this period is pitifully inadequate. It seems valid, however, to suggest that

Date B.C.	Northern or Lower Egypt	Southern or Upper Egypt	Main Sites	Period
c. 3600	Maadi	Early Gerzean	el-Maadi	Middle and Late Predynastic
c. 3400	Late Gerzean		el-Gerza, Haraga	
c. 3200	The Union of Upper and Lower Egypt under one king		Hierakonpolis Memphis Abydos	Historic

Table B   Later Prehistoric Period

most of these innovations came through a sudden intensifica-
tion of culture-contacts in the Eastern Mediterranean as a
result of the invention of the sea-going ship, a factor which
may have induced the almost simultaneous flowering of the
Cretan and Egyptian civilizations. The development of
wooden ships able to sail the tideless Mediterranean must have
occurred outside Egypt in a large timber-growing area with
an extensive seaboard, and the evidence points to Byblos
in the Lebanon as the centre of this new industry. Trading
contacts would be quite sufficient to account for an enhanced
infiltration of different ideas and techniques which could be
adapted by the Egyptians to their own peculiar conditions. It
was at this point that a Mediterranean Bronze Age culture was
grafted on to a native African stock to produce the essential
Egyptian civilization. The isolation of Egypt in the Near East
during ancient times has been much exaggerated. She shared
a common trade, technology, and material culture with her
neighbours and while strongly influenced by them, also
influenced them in turn. The distinctive character that her
civilization took was almost entirely due to its political
institutions and these as we shall see came from an African
component.

The Late Predynastic cultures of this second phase have
been identified at el-Gerza and other sites in the Faiyum, and
found superseding the Amratian cultures at Nagada and

el-Ballas near Koptos. The transition to the Early Dynastic style of historic Egypt is thereafter progressive. The pottery includes wavy-handled jars, similar to those found in Palestine, and a light pink or buff ware painted in red with such motifs as primitive shrines, emblems probably representing deities, plants, animals, and human figures. Some pots are shaped and decorated to simulate the stone vases that now become common probably because of the introduction of a cranked flint-borer. The working of flint itself achieves an unrivalled perfection, knives of thin section being produced with regu-

Plate 2

larly ripple-flaked blades. In this mastery over material the Egyptians were already displaying that superb technical skill, particularly over intractable substances, that distinguishes their best work from that of other nations of Antiquity.

In the Late Gerzean period from about 3400 to 3200 B.C. there is evidence of increased political activity and the general opinion is that a struggle for predominance now developed between Upper and Lower Egypt. In both regions the basic unit of government was the local community clustered around a town or group of villages, under the aegis of a local variant of one of the universal gods, and looking for leadership to some powerful headman. These districts or *nomes*, as the Greeks called them, were the smallest fragments into which the country naturally splintered in times of anarchy. It is to be presumed, however, that the city-states of the Delta were more advanced, independent, and jealous of their local traditions than the simpler folk-communities of Upper Egypt, and more difficult to weld into a corporate whole. We may perhaps trace even in Late Gerzean times the first emergence of a pattern that occurs again and again in Egyptian history—it is always from the South that an ambitious prince arises who puts an end to a period of anarchy by combining the districts of Upper Egypt under his sway and swallowing piecemeal the local rulers of the North, so creating one State out of a congeries of

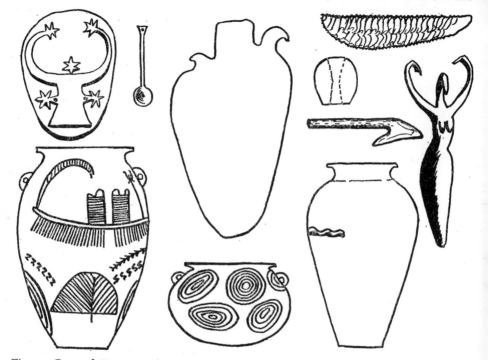

Fig. 19   Group of Gerzean artifacts: pottery with red designs on buff; slate palettes, one with the head of Hathor as the celestial cow; ivory spoon; pottery figurine of a dancer; ripple-flaked flint knife; piriform stone mace-head; copper harpoon-head; c. 3300 B.C.

rival powers. The character of the unification of Egypt at the beginning of the Middle Kingdom, the New Kingdom, and the Ethiopian Dynasty XXV may perhaps suggest how this unity was achieved for the first time at the dawn of the Dynastic Age.

The evidence for the political ferment which produced Dynastic Egypt is contained in a number of votive objects, particularly palettes and mace-heads, which have been excavated at Hierakonpolis and which will be discussed in a later chapter. Here we may limit our examination to remarking

Plate 5

Fig. 45

73

the appearance of rudimentary hieroglyphs on some of these antiquities, showing that we now have to do with the written documents of a civilized State.

4. THE ARCHAIC PERIOD
Dynasties I and II, c. 3200–2660 B.C.

Plate 5

The unification of Egypt was traditionally ascribed to Menes the first Pharaoh, whom Egyptologists equate with Narmer (or perhaps Merinar), a king whose monuments have been found at Hierakonpolis and Abydos near which the dynasty originated. The material remains of this period are scanty and come mostly from greatly damaged tombs at Saqqara and the no less ruined cenotaphs at Abydos. Perhaps if our picture were more complete we should be able to see that the transition from the culture of Predynastic to that of Pharaonic Egypt was gradual, but at this distance of time, it has all the appearance of a sudden efflorescence. It may be that the cessation of sectarian strife and the concentration of effort under one leader stimulated a great upsurge in all manner of creative enterprises.

According to a tradition which Herodotus records, Menes was accredited with founding 'White Walls' as a Residence City, later to be called Memphis, on ground reclaimed by diverting the course of the Nile at the junction of Upper and Lower Egypt. He also undertook larger irrigation and drainage schemes in the vicinity, a policy to which subsequent kings must have been committed by the magical powers they were supposed to exercise over the Nile flood, and by the demands of a growing population. A steadily increasing prosperity is to be inferred from the progressive size and magnificence of the tombs of this dynasty. The large timber joists and roofing beams used in these constructions suggest that trade with the

c. 3050 B.C.

Lebanon was extensive. A rock-relief of Djer the third king of the dynasty has come to light near Buhen in the Sudan and

Approx. Date B.C.	Principal Kings	Funerary Customs	Significant Events
3200	DYNASTY I Menes (Narmer) Ity I (Hor-Àha) Ity II (Djer) Merbiapen (Adjib)	Royal burials in main tomb at Saqqara Cenotaphs at Abydos	Development of writing, copper tools and weapons Trade with Levant Expeditions to Sudan
2900 2660	DYNASTY II Hetep-sekhem-wy Neb-re Ni-neter Peribsen Kha-sekhem-wy	Private burials near tomb or cenotaph of the king	Use of stone in building and for statuary Religious and political strife Pacification of the Two Lands

Table C Archaic Period (Dynasties I and II)

shows that some attempt was already being made to control the savage tribes even of this remote Southern region, probably by armed forays.

The monuments of Dynasty II are even scantier than those of Dynasty I. The Royal tombs of the period have not yet been found though they probably await discovery under the Saqqara sands. Cenotaphs have, however, been uncovered by Petrie at Abydos. It would appear that, as so often happens in Egyptian history, the new rulers were inimical to the family they supplanted. An echo of rebellion and religious strife is faintly caught in the fragmentary records that have survived. All the tombs and cenotaphs of Dynasty I have been deliber- ately and openly fired, and of the rich treasure that they once contained only a few tantalizing scraps exist. This contention at the very head of affairs must have retarded the growth of the Pharaonic State and reduced its prestige and prosperity. An end to discord came, however, with the advent of a Southerner,

Plate 4
Fig. 21

Fig. 20   Line-drawing from part of a relief on the rocks near Buhen showing Nubian foes fallen in battle and a pinioned captive tied to the prow of a ship. The personification of Nubia is led captive before the king's name; the two wheel-like glyphs represent captured towns; reign of King Djer; c. 3020 B.C.

<table>
<tr><td>c. 2670 B.C.</td></tr>
</table>

c. 2670 B.C.

Kha-sekhem-wy, who reconciled the two warring factions and reunited the country under his sole rule. His son was the first king of Dynasty III and with him the Golden Age of the Old Kingdom gets fairly into its stride.

The Archaic Period of the first two dynasties awaits further archaeological investigation but can hardly be fully revealed to us. Its literary records are few and their interpretation is highly tentative. We are largely dependent therefore upon fragmentary material remains in assessing the extent of the cultural achievement. Such a traditional craft as the working of stone into vessels continues with unabated zest, banded alabasters, porphyries, breccias, diorites, and similar stones being selected for their attractive formations. Occasionally a painstaking virtuosity is displayed in the carving of fanciful

Plate 3

trays and dishes, imitating leaf forms or metal prototypes. In contrast, pottery loses the fine shapes and finishes of the Predynastic wares, and becomes merely utilitarian, probably with the introduction of the potter's wheel at the beginning of the period. The working of copper, on the other hand, was greatly expanded. A rich hoard of copper tools, weapons, and ingots was found in one of the royal tombs at Saqqara, which also contained bowls, ewers, and vases, raised by hammering copper sheets on wooden stakes. These are the forerunners of

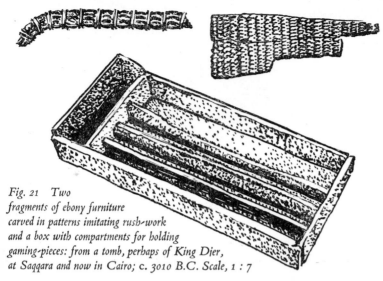

*Fig. 21 Two
fragments of ebony furniture
carved in patterns imitating rush-work
and a box with compartments for holding
gaming-pieces: from a tomb, perhaps of King Dier,
at Saqqara and now in Cairo; c. 3010 B.C. Scale, 1 : 7*

a long sequence of metal vessels which were produced at all
periods in Ancient Egypt. Gold vessels of similar type, but
probably more elaborate work, must also have existed in these
early deposits but have not escaped the greedy eye of the
tomb-robber. Copper was used for other purposes at this
period since the Palermo Stone mentions the making of statues
of Kha-sekhem-wy in copper. These were almost certainly of
wood with sheets of copper hammered over them similar to
two life-sized Royal statues of Phiops I and his little son
which have survived from Dynasty VI at Hierakonpolis in a
damaged and corroded state. An increasing boldness in the
working of copper throughout the Archaic Period and Early
Old Kingdom is, in fact, a concomitant of progressive
technological skill: it has been computed, for instance, that
the large granite sarcophagi of Dynasty IV must have been
cut with copper saws over eight feet long, using quartz sand
as an abrasive.

From the debris of the Royal tombs of the Archaic Period

cf. Fig. 15
Plate 19

Plate 4

have been recovered exquisitely worked fragments of ivory, ebony, and other woods, revealing a high standard of luxury in domestic equipment. It is clear, however, that much of this material is but a version in more durable and expensive materials of archetypes in rush-work and basketry. But a severely proportioned box divided into compartments which has survived almost intact is constructed strictly according to the functional qualities of timber, showing that the exploitation of wood for its own sake was well understood.

In all this work in metal, ivory, and wood, Egyptian crafts-men were probably influenced by ideas and techniques common to the Eastern Mediterranean, but there are some inventions of this period for which an Egyptian origin may confidently be claimed. The first is a plastic substance, usually referred to as Egyptian faience, which was evidently developed by a people living on the Libyan border after which it was named. This material, made of crushed quartz pebbles, could be cast, carved, shaped, and fired to produce a substance like brilliant blue or green glazed pottery. In this craft Egypt re-mained pre-eminent during her long history, subsequently developing white, yellow, violet, red, and black glazes and producing wares in two or more colours. Objects in faience range from beads and inlays to statues and a giant votive sceptre, but the majority of pieces are vessels, some of them worked with great artistry. The second craft which Egypt made peculiarly her own was stone-working. Even during the Early Predynastic Period vessels were crudely ground out of soft and hard stones, but from the Archaic Age onwards not only are special rocks sought from which to fashion objects of beauty as well as utility, but larger granite boulders also are shaped into sills, lintels, jambs, and other constructional members. Statues too are now hewn in granites and slate as well as the softer limestones.

Plates 28, 64, 68, 72

The third material, and perhaps the most important for

Fig. 22   A steward reads out an inventory from a papyrus roll which his scribes with palettes, pointed erasers on cords, water-pots, pens and portfolios have prepared; from a relief in the tomb of Mereruka at Saqqara; c. 2330 B.C. Scale, 1 : 4

which an Egyptian origin may be claimed is papyrus, a flexible paper made from the pith of the papyrus plant and known from the very beginning of historical times at least. For use with this paper, and also with the leather rolls that were employed for more permanent records, a rush pen, cut to a chisel point, and black and red inks were invented. A rapid and cursive system of writing, adapted to the use of such materials, underwent its own continuous development for as long as the Egyptian language was spoken. The Ancient Egyptians thus had from the start a convenient means for noting, computing, and documenting all the business of State. Records could be kept in portable and durable form, dupli- cated at will, and not entrusted to fallible human memory.

Figs. 3, 48

79

c. 2270 B.C.

Precise instructions could be issued at a distance and reports received from afar. The classic example of the system in action during the Old Kingdom is the correspondence between the young king Phiops II and the explorer Harkhuf, who on his return from his fourth expedition into the Sudan, had written to the King reporting his arrival at Aswan and the bringing back of a dancing pygmy similar to the creature brought home from Punt by a certain Ba⁄wer⁄djed a century earlier. The King wrote to Harkhuf giving detailed instructions for him to come to the Court immediately bringing the remarkable pygmy with him in care of reliable attendants, and saying that if Harkhuf arrived with his charge in good health and spirits, he would reward him even more generously than Ba⁄wer⁄djed had been treated.

Without the instrument of writing, the highly organized administration of the Egyptian State would not have been possible: in fact the creation of a unified Government may well have had to await the invention and spread of writing.

With the art of writing there was a parallel development in the science of calculation. A decimal system had existed in Predynastic times and it is probable that during the Archaic Period nearly all the edifice of later Egyptian mathematics was raised on this foundation. The motive force was purely utilitarian, the need for solving the many practical problems that faced a centralized State dependent for its wealth upon a system of taxation. The inundations of the Nile often swept away old landmarks and an accurate survey had periodically to be made to re⁄establish former boundaries according to the written records. While linear measure, like that of Europe before the introduction of the metric system, was based upon the dimensions of the human body, the finger, palm, forearm, and so forth, measures of capacity also existed for assessing the amount of the corn, wine, and oil harvests. In the important tomb of Hesi⁄re, an official of King Djoser of Early Dynasty III,

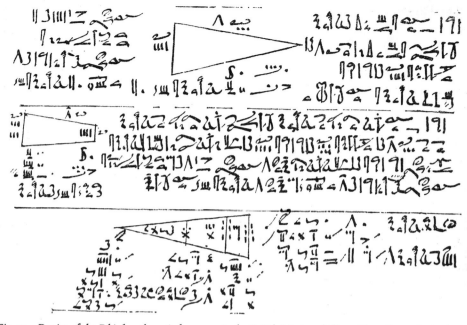

Fig. 23 Portion of the Rhind mathematical papyrus in the British Museum dealing with problems of triangles; c. 1600 B.C. Scale, 1 : 2

two elaborate sets of fourteen wooden and leather tubs with strikers for measuring his rents in corn, are included among other essential equipment painted on the chapel wall.

The science of computing time did not lag behind that of measuring space. The prosperity of an agricultural community depended upon forecasting the annual rise of the Nile and its probable volume, and what in a pre-scientific society was just as important, the auspicious moment for a feast or religious ceremony to ensure the success of an undertaking. The Predynastic Egyptian camping out under his brilliant night sky could hardly fail to observe recurring celestial phenomena such as the heliacal rising of stars on the horizon as a means of dividing time into sequences. Astronomy was studied at Heliopolis, the centre of the sun-cult, the ritual of which was intimately concerned with time-measurement and the movements of heavenly bodies. Architects and engineers of Heliopolitan origin may well have been responsible for the extremely accurate orientation of pyramids and their geometrical perfection during the Early Old Kingdom. The Archaic Period saw the introduction of a more accurate calendar, based upon twelve months each of thirty days with five intercalary feast-days, to supplement the old agricultural lunar calendar which had persisted from Predynastic times. A third even more accurate calendar was later adopted *c.* 2500 B.C. with the full ascendancy of Heliopolis.

During the four centuries of the Archaic Period there was an evident ferment in all fields of endeavour, and some scholars have claimed to detect in it a fumbling towards a scientific attitude on the part of the Ancient Egyptian in an organized world which he was having to establish as much by processes of ratiocination as by trial and error. Two literary works, which from internal evidence are thought to originate in the time of Dynasty I, are the warrant for this viewpoint. The first is a treatise upon surgery, especially fractures, known as the Edwin Smith Papyrus, which is remarkable for its empirical approach and is not paralleled by subsequent medical writings in Ancient Egypt. Manetho records that the second king of the dynasty was a noted physician and wrote works on anatomy. The other work is a theological composition ascribing the creation of the universe to Ptah in which a novel search for first principles is evident. According to tradition the cult of Ptah was founded at Memphis by Menes and it may be that the same processes were at work in the creation of the syncretic Memphite theology as in the formation of the Egyptian State. But however scientific this approach may have been, it was short-lived: the consolidation of Egyptian culture in the next period ensured that an end was put to experiment.

*24 Wooden corn-
with striker, after a
ting in the tomb-
nel of Hesi-re at Saq-
; c. 2650 B.C. Scale
7*

Plate 24

Chapter V

The First Flowering during the Old Kingdom

Dynasties III–VI, c. 2660–2180 B.C.

THE GROWTH MADE in the first two dynasties comes into full flower during the next two. Different reliefs near the tur-quoise and copper-ore mines in Sinai show us the aggressive Armenoid features of Sa-nakht and his brother Djoser smiting the traditional Bedouin of the locality; but it is rather in the arts of peace that Dynasty III made its mark and here the hero was not a king but a king's man, the Vizier Imhotep, wise in the learning of Heliopolis. In Imhotep we can recognize the first known genius of historic times whose thought and imagination transcended his age and steered the course of human culture into new channels. In later periods, he was celebrated as an astronomer, architect, writer, sage, and above all as a physician, being eventually deified as the god of medicine whom the Greeks called Imuthes. While his cult belongs to the Late Period and smacks a little of the apocryphal, a statue-base of King Djoser has come to light at Saqqara bearing the name and titles of Imhotep upon it and testifying to the weight of the legend. Today Imhotep's greatest memorial is undoubtedly the vast monument he raised for Djoser at Saqqara and which we call the Step Pyramid. *c.* 4th cent. B.C.

Since Prehistoric times building had advanced from the mud hovels and reed windbreaks that still sheltered a peasantry whose life was spent mostly in the open. The introduction of mud-brick and imported timbers wrought great changes in architectural design and methods, though many decorative adjuncts were still determined by an older form of construction using lashed bundles of papyrus stalks, mat-work hangings, palm-thatch, and wattle and daub. In the Archaic Period, however, stone begins to be used for parts of the buildings

Date B.C. and Years of Reign	Principal Kings	Main Sites	Funerary Customs	Significant Events
c. 2660	DYNASTY III			
	Sa-nakht		Royal burial in	Large-scale
19	Neter-khet (Djoser)	Saqqara	Step Pyramid	building and
6	Sekhem-khet	Sinai	Private mastabas	sculpture in
24	Huny		near Royal tomb	stone
			(Hesi-re, Methen)	
c. 2600	DYNASTY IV			
			Evolution of true	Great technical
24	Sneferu	Maidum	pyramid and	and artistic
23	Khufu (Kheops)	Dahshur	climax of its	mastery over
31	Khafra (Khephren)	Giza	development	most materials
18	Menkaure (Mykerinus)	Bubastis	Private burial	The classic
			in mastabas and	age of the Old
			some rock-tombs	Kingdom
c. 2500				

Table D   Old Kingdom (Dynasties III and IV)

subjected to hard wear; but the logical step of constructing entirely in stone was not taken even for the 'eternal habitations' of the Royal dead until the reign of Djoser. A monumental conception of architecture arose in Egypt through the necessity of housing the dead King in a tomb that would endure for ever.

Although there is a reference to the building of a temple in stone during the reign of Kha-sekhem-wy, and one of his funerary chambers was lined with cut limestone, the art of building in stone was traditionally attributed to Imhotep; and certainly his Step Pyramid is the earliest sizable stone structure raised by man in the entire world. The actual tomb of Djoser, and perhaps also that of his predecessor Sa-nakht, were beneath a giant stone staircase of six stages reaching towards the sky-realms for a height of over two hundred feet. This stepped

Plate 6

pyramid was surrounded by various courts and buildings, the whole enclosed by a massive bastioned girdle-wall with a perimeter of over a mile and a height of more than thirty feet, imitating perhaps the white walls of Memphis, and forming a veritable Residence City of the dead King.

In the Archaic Period the royal tombs took the form of a true sepulchre at Saqqara, apparently modelled on the Lower Egyptian house of the living, and a cenotaph at Abydos, based on the sepulchral mound of Upper Egypt. In Djoser's funerary

Fig. 25 King Sa-nakht wearing the White Crown of Upper Egypt and holding sceptres, after a relief on the rocks in the Wadi Maghara, Sinai; c. 2665 B.C. Scale, 1 : 5

monument the giant tomb-mound becomes a stepped super-structure, perhaps under the influence of Heliopolitan ideas, while associated with it in the same complex is a series of buildings imitating the houses of the living. We thus see architectural expression given to an integration of comple-mentary ideas which in the sphere of politics was the result of Kha-sekhem-wy's reconciliation of opposing factions. Later in the Old Kingdom, the Pharaoh was to be buried in a stone mound in a sarcophagus decorated as a palace building.

The Step Pyramid displays many features which reveal that the architect was feeling his way in an unfamiliar medium.

Fig. 26 Rebuilt entrance-port in the 30-ft-high girdle wall of the Step Pyramid of King Djoser at Saqqara; c. 2650 B.C.

The slender elegant proportions of the ancillary buildings, and many decorative elements, are proper to construction in mud and vegetable products, and the small-block limestone masonry suggests a brick archetype. Nevertheless, from the time of its erection this monument must have been the wonder of its age and spread Egypt's fame afar. It preserved within its confines a museum of choice objects from ribbed wall-panels of blue-glazed tiles imitating coloured mat-hangings, large seated and standing statues of the King, stelae in delicate low relief showing Djoser in some eternal jubilee, and over thirty thousand handsome stone vessels of every shape and size. In addition to all this, of course, was that more costly treasure which has doubtless been pillaged from it long ago.

Plate 7

The rapidity with which the technique of building in stone developed in Egypt is seen in the similar but unfinished complex of Djoser's successor, Sekhem-khet, which has recently been uncovered near by. This monument is built in much more massive masonry which has lost all resemblance to a mud brick original. The use of large limestone blocks becomes ever bolder in the subsequent funerary structures that were raised during the next century or so by the kings of Dynasty IV who at Dahshur, Maidum, and Giza built giant stone pyramids as tombs. The climax of this development was reached with the construction of the Great Pyramid of Kheops at Giza when well over two million blocks of limestone, some of them weighing fifteen tons apiece, were hauled up ramps flanking each side of the base to form a stupendous monument built to extremely fine limits of accuracy. The core blocks were quarried on the spot, but the casing stones of fine lime stone were cut at Tura, across the river, and ferried over to the working face in the season of high Nile. In addition, granite boulders were hewn as jambs and relieving beams. The quarrying of hard stones had become sufficiently advanced by the reign of Mykerinus for the lower courses of his pyramid, the smallest of the Giza trio, to be cased with red granite. All

c. 2590 B.C.

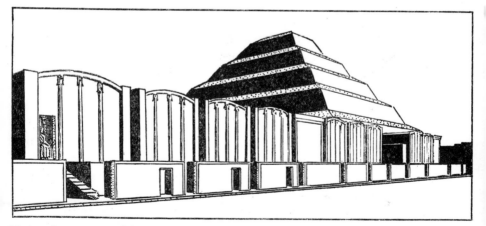

Fig. 27   Reconstruction of the Court of the Jubilee Festival flanked on two sides by dummy chapels; the Step Pyramid, Saqqara, c. 2650 B.C.

cf. *Fig. 29*

three pyramids had their subsidiary pyramids and mortuary buildings enclosed within a girdle-wall and connected by a covered causeway to a temple near the limits of the Nile flood. Some scholars believe that these Valley temples were but massive versions in stone of a prehistoric tent of light poles and matting in which to the chanting of funerary prayers the corpses of the kings were probably purified and embalmed. The dilapidated and undecorated state in which the Giza monuments have come down to us leaves an impression of stark austerity, though from Herodotus' remarks it is clear that the pyramid causeways at Giza were decorated with reliefs in very much the same manner as that found in later complexes, notably of Wenis of Dynasty V at Saqqara. Nevertheless, the Valley

Plate 17

temple of Khephren which is the best preserved of the ancillary buildings at Giza must have been tremendously impressive in its original state with the sunlight streaming through louvres cut below the red granite ceiling and falling upon the polished alabaster floor and scattering a diffused glow upon the twenty-

Plate 9

three statues of the King carved from alabasters, greywackes, and green diorites that stood before the red granite piers. In the uncompromising severity and nicely calculated effects of this, the most complete realization of the mortuary concept in Ancient Egyptian architecture, we see the same intelligence at work that raised the pyramids of Giza in all their accuracy and orientated them with great precision. In the impressive

Plate 11

portrait statue of Kheops' cousin, the Vizier Hemon ('the Devotee of Heliopolis'), who was evidently responsible for the building of the Great Pyramid, there is more than a hint of that divine assurance and intellectual ruthlessness which these early engineers must have possessed in such abundance to plan, organize, and carry out such mighty works.

Plates 8, 9, 12

   The Giza monuments, no less than others of their kind, were repositories of statuary, reliefs, furniture, vessels, and other funerary equipment upon which the best artists of the day

Fig. 28   Granite piers and architraves in the main hall of the Valley Temple of the Second Pyramid of Khephren at Giza; c. 2525 B.C.

were encouraged to lavish their talents. Most of it has been destroyed without trace, but we are fortunate that some samples have survived of the brilliant art of this classic period of Egypt's past. In particular, the painstaking work of the Boston archaeologists has succeeded in accurately reconstructing the magnificent furniture of Queen Hetep-heres, the mother of Kheops, from her greatly decayed secondary burial. The superb design, proportions, and workmanship of these boxes, chairs, bed, and canopy with their fine work in carved ebony and cedar wood, their overlays of moulded, chased, and engraved gold and their inlays of blue and black faience and red carnelian, display a taste that is both highly luxurious yet under perfect restraint.

Plate 8

Date B.C. and Years of Reign	Principal Kings	Main Sites	Funerary Customs	Significant Events
c. 2500	DYNASTY V		Royal pyramids smaller, but adjuncts decor- ated with fine reliefs	Rise in import- ance of Heliopolis
8	Weser-kaf			
15	Sahu-re	Saqqara		
11	Ne-weser-re	Abusir		Expeditions
28	Djed-ka-re Isesi	Heliopolis		to Punt
30	Wenis		*Pyramid Texts*	Private sculpture in wood and stone of high standard
			Gradual increase in size of private mastabas (Ti, Mereruka)	
c. 2340	DYNASTY VI			Decentralization of government
15	Teti	Deir el-Gebrawi		
44	Pepy I (Phiops I)	Koptos	Rock-tombs in provincial centres	
5	Mer-en-re I	Abydos		Rise in feudal- ism, leading to anarchy
90	Pepy II (Phiops II)	Saqqara		
c. 2180				

Table E Later Old Kingdom (Dynasties V and VI)

The heavy drain upon human and material resources that the building of the Giza pyramids must have imposed was not demanded of their subjects by later Pharaohs. The pyramids of the kings of Dynasties V and VI were built at Abusir and Saqqara on a very much humbler scale and to very much lower standards, which is why they exist today as mere mounds of debris. The decline in the size of the king's tomb is matched by a shrinking in the stature of the Pharaoh and an increase in the influence of Heliopolis and its sun-god Re. The Pharaoh, so far from being a mighty god in his own right, is now but the son of a great divinity. At death he no longer bursts into the sky-realms as a cannibal hunter, lassoing the gods and butchering them like cattle for his cooking-pots.

Fig. 29   Reconstruction of the pyramid complexes of Nefer-ir-ka-re, Ne-weser-re and Sahu-re at Abusir. The complex of Nefer-ir-ka-re was incomplete at his death and the causeway was later adapted by Ne-weser-re for his own pyramid. In the far distance are the sun-temples of Weser-kaf and Ne-weser-re, Dynasty V; c. 2490-2410 B.C.

Instead he begs to be ferried across the waters of the underworld to act as a secretary to Re, or as a rower in the solar barque.

The ritual of the sun-cult centred about a squat obelisk in an open court, and this may have influenced the architecture of the period, which loses the massiveness of the Dynasty IV style and becomes light and vital with such naturalistic elements as columns in the form of date-palms or clusters of papyrus stalks. Above all, the lavish decoration of the temples with delicate reliefs introduces a number of subjects which, fragmentary though they may be, appear to be new and inspired by the preoccupation of the sun-cult with the calendar and time-measurement. A common theme is the personification of the three seasons, Inundation, Winter, and Spring, with their appropriate plants and animals. A complete cycle of agricultural labour from sowing to reaping is represented as a

Plate 16

91

Fig. 30   Reconstruction of the sun-temple of Ne-weser-re at Abu Ghurab opposite Heli
a pedestal. Painted reliefs decorated the walls of the causeway corridor, the east and south si

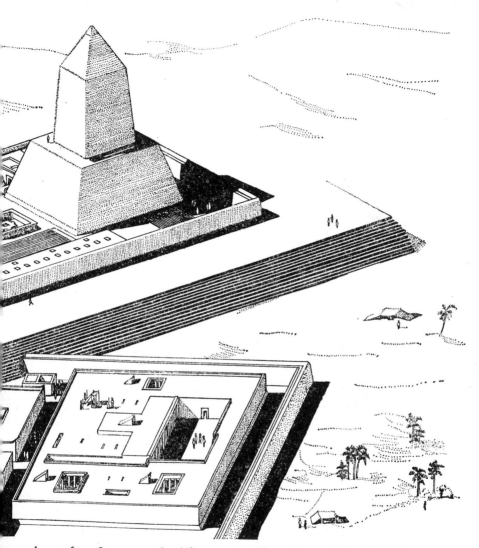

e central court of over 80,000 square feet, before a massive alabaster altar, stands the obelisk of the sun-cult on *d a cult-chapel; c. 2430 B.C.*

sort of visual anthem to the sun-god for all its gifts. The use
of polished basalts, granites, and alabasters in the construction
of the pyramid-temples, however, continues the tradition of
the preceding dynasty. The great monument of the Pyramid

Age is the complex of Phiops II which, although now in a
greatly dilapidated condition, has surrendered enough evidence
to show that this edifice, with its elaborate valley building,
causeway, and mortuary temple, all decorated with a wealth
of painted reliefs, was the most developed version of the Old
Kingdom pyramid-tomb. In later years it seems to have
gathered a special importance as the final classic utterance of
the Old Kingdom. Its reliefs were copied both in style and
substance by the Pharaohs of the Middle and New Kingdoms,
anxious to return to the traditions of a past which seemed the
more glorious by contrast with what had followed it.

The grandiose funerary projects of the kings of Dynasty IV
absorbed all the artistic ability of the day. It is true that at Giza
the kings planned and equipped large mastaba-tombs around
their pyramids for the faithful officials who were also their

Plate 11

close relatives; but apart from the statue of Hemon, which
belongs really to the traditions of the preceding reign, very little
private sculpture of this period has survived, unless one includes the so-called reserve-heads buried with the deceased
perhaps as a magic substitute. It may be that statues of private
persons were not provided for the funerary chambers; and the
most ambitious piece of private sculpture surviving from this

Plate 10

period, the bust of the vizier Ankh-haf, a brother of Kheops,
carved in the austere tradition of the reserve-heads, may have
been used in the funerary ritual and not intended as a tomb-
statue. The chief products of the studios destined for non-Royal
use were reliefs for insertion in the brick offering-niches built
against the east face of the Giza mastabas, the main feature of
the decoration being a painted slab showing the owner seated
before a table of offerings. These slab-stelae with their lists of

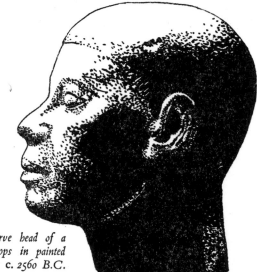

Fig. 31 So-called reserve head of a daughter-in-law of Kheops in painted limestone, now in Boston; c. 2560 B.C. Height 12 in.

equipment were given to their courtiers by the Pharaohs almost as a certificate of ownership; and though in ensuing centuries the offering-niche was to be expanded into a stone chapel, often of large dimensions with walls covered with painted reliefs and with the central feature of a false portal, the essential offering-stela still remained the focal-point.

Plate 15

By the end of Dynasty IV several generations of sculptors had developed the classical art of Kheops into a hereditary craft, and with the far less ambitious programmes of the sun-kings of the Dynasties V and VI a reserve of talent became available for work on the private tomb-chapels at Saqqara. Most of these commissions, however, were still at the behest of the king. Sahu-re, for instance, decreed that the High Priest of Memphis and his craftsmen should make a double tomb-portal for his chief physician, and the work was done in the audience-chamber of the palace under the daily inspection of

c. 2480 B.C.

Fig. 32 Idy enjoys a picnic while on a fishing excursion, from a relief in the tomb of Mereruka at Saqqara; c. 2330 B.C. Scale, 1 : 5.

the King himself. It is upon the private statuary and the mastaba-reliefs of Dynasties V and VI that we are largely dependent for our estimate of the standard of material culture attained by the Egyptians in the Pyramid Age, since the Royal monuments are in so ruinous a condition. In particular the large mastaba-chapels of the Curator of Monuments, Ti, of Dynasty V, and of the Governor of Memphis, Mereruka, of Dynasty VI, both at Saqqara, allow us more than a passing glimpse into the busy and assured world of the large estate of the period—the cycle of work in its fields, the country crafts, the hunting and fishing in *wadi* and marsh, the boating or the picnic on the river, the music, dancing, feasting, and children's games, and the humorous and kindly observation of the foibles

Plate 18

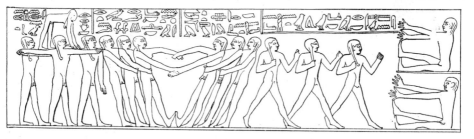

Fig. 33   Children playing at pick-a-back, tug-of-war, and a kind of leapfrog still practised in Nubia, from a relief in the tomb of Mereruka at Saqqara; c. 2330 B.C. Scale, 1 : 12.

of the peasantry, their bald heads and ill-shaven jowls, their trouble with the refractory ass or the no less adamant tax-collector, their work-songs, their banter. The statuary, too, in painted wood and limestone shows the same sardonic dis-tinction between an *élite* which is athletic in youth, sleek and well-fed in maturity, confident and successful at all ages, and its servants who are often scraggy and undersized and a little clownish. Since there are statues, however, of important persons who were unflatteringly represented as a dwarf or hunchback, we must assume that the mirror which the artist held up to nature was not always a distorting-glass.

Plates 13, 14

While thus our image of internal conditions in Egypt seems sharply in focus, our knowledge of her foreign relations during this period is far more indistinct. Some control was evidently exercised over Nubia and the Upper Sudan, largely for trading purposes and for the recruitment of fighting-men like the Medjay folk (later synonymous with 'police'); but it is doubtful whether the Egyptians were able to subdue for long the warlike though more primitive tribes of the Sudan who had the advantage of inhabiting a difficult terrain through which even progress by boat was hazardous. Towards the end of the Old Kingdom the frontier was kept by powerful border barons, or Governors of the South, like Weni and Harkhuf. Trading ventures by sea to the mysterious spice-lands of Punt, thought

Plate 21

cf. *Fig. 40*

to be on the Somali coast, were undertaken for the sake of the incense gums and resins demanded by temple ritual. We have references to expeditions sent in Dynasties V and VI, though earlier voyages must surely have been made. Mining operations in Sinai and the Arabian desert were often threatened by the local Bedouin who doubtless interrupted communications and had to be harried from time to time. The Libyans on the western border were also traditional skirmishers, though it is not certain if damaged scenes in the temples of Sahu⁄re, Wenis, and Phiops II, showing the king taking booty from them, are not mythical and do not refer to events dating back to the dawn of history.

There is rather more evidence for Egyptian penetration in Palestine. Two representations have survived in different tombs showing the storming of Asiatic fortresses, and the autobiography which Weni inscribed in his tomb⁄chapel at Abydos describes a series of ambitious campaigns including a combined operation which he organized and led into Palestine as far north as Carmel during the reign of Phiops I. The most impressive testimony for Egyptian activity abroad, however, comes from the Byblos region in the Lebanon where a fragment of a stone vase inscribed with the name of Kha⁄sekhem⁄wy, and objects bearing the cartouches of Kheops and Mykerinus have been brought to light. As early as Dynasty IV a temple appears to have been built there, perhaps for the benefit of an Egyptian community. Byblos was the great port for the timber trade of the Lebanon and a centre for commerce from all lands of the Eastern Mediterranean, and it was probably through peaceful trading contacts, rather than conquest, that Egypt wielded such influence in this important city⁄state. A damaged gold⁄covered throne bearing the names of Sahu⁄re has been found as far afield as northern Anatolia, though whether it was acquired directly by trade or by plunder⁄ing some Syrian princeling is unknown.

c. 2300 B.C.

Fig. 34   Soldiers storm a fortress-city with a scaling-ladder; others undermine the foundations and lead off captives; within the city, women grapple with invaders while their ruler tears his hair in despair; after a tomb-relief at Dishasha, south of Herakleopolis; c. 2370 B.C. Scale, 1 : 13.

From the time of Menes it would seem that the Pharaoh ruled over the whole of Egypt as his demesne, and even in Dynasty IV the system still prevailed, with the king's palace and its adjoining official quarters acting as the 'Great House' where the government of the country was conducted by chosen ministers to whom Royal authority had been delegated. Most of these officials were sons or relatives of the kings who saw to their upbringing and education, maintained them during life, and granted them decent burial on death. This highly cen-tralized organization began to decay in the later years of

Dynasty IV as provincial governorships and other posts were accepted as hereditary appointments. At the same time favoured courtiers were rewarded with gifts of land as endowments for the upkeep of their tombs and funerary services. Such gifts were often exempted from taxation in perpetuity, and the vast silent cities of the dead, around the pyramids of their former lords, received large shares of the national resources at the expense of the Royal Exchequer. Much of this expenditure was upon unproductive activities, such as the chanting of funerary prayers, which only encouraged economic stagnation. The district governors, once secure in their hereditary posts, handed on their offices to their sons in the firm belief that they owed their appointments by right of birth and not by favour of the king. They no longer sought burial near the Royal pyramid but made their own rock-tombs at the provincial capital, like so many minor kings, importing craftsmen where necessary from Memphis. The stature of the Pharaoh had already shrunk during the rise of the Heliopolitan sun-cult. It suffered further diminution when the great chasm that separated the divine king from human-kind was spanned by the marriage of the Pharaoh to women of non-Royal blood, as happened most notably with Phiops I in the later part of his reign. By the middle of Dynasty VI, Egypt was almost back to the state from which Menes had rescued her, a federation of feudal potentates each governing his own district for its benefit alone. Only the original momentum and prestige of the monarchy kept the system working, but the *coup de grâce* was administered during the long reign of Phiops II, who ruled for over ninety years and died a centenarian. At his death, the central power was too weak and divided to hold back the surging tide of anarchy, and the civilization of the Old Kingdom was swept away with the political system that had created it.

Egypt during the Old Kingdom evolved a virile and

self-assured culture which is perhaps her most characteristic expression. The calm faces that gaze out from so many statues and reliefs are untroubled by doubts, and the voices which speak from the scanty writings of the period, the books of precepts and the autobiographies, are unfaltering in their belief that the good life consisted in being modest, discreet, honest, and patient; prudent in friendship, not covetous, nor envious; but paying proper respect to superiors: in short, keeping one's proper station and exercising moderation in all things. Such an ideal of the golden mean was essentially aristocratic. The King and his Court, mostly officials of Royal descent who proclaimed their kinship with the Pharaoh and partook in some degree of his immortality, were the *élite* for whom the economic and artistic enterprises of the State were created. But while forming a privileged class they were no idle Court nobility. They comprised the architects, writers, theologians, administrators—all the men of action and intelligence in their day.

CHAPTER VI

The First Breakdown and Recovery during the Middle Kingdom

I. THE FIRST INTERMEDIATE PERIOD

Dynasties VII–X, c. 2180–2080 B.C.

THE CONDITIONS PREVAILING at the collapse of Dynasty VI have been vividly described in a papyrus at Leyden known to Egyptologists as *The Admonitions of the Prophet Ipuwer.* In this work, Ipuwer upbraids an unnamed king for his supinity while the country falls to ruin, and shows something of an unholy relish in cataloguing all the miseries that have beset the land:

> The high-born are full of lamentation but the poor are jubilant. Every town sayeth, 'Let us drive out the powerful'. . . . The splendid judgement-hall has been stripped of its documents. . . . The public offices lie open and their records have been stolen. Serfs have become the masters of serfs. . . . Behold, they that had clothes are now in rags. . . . He who had nothing is now rich and the high official must court the parvenu. . . . Squalor is throughout the land: no clothes are white these days. . . . The Nile is in flood yet no one has the heart to plough. . . . Corn has perished every-where. . . . People are stripped of clothing, perfume, and oil. . . . Everyone says, 'There is no more'. . . . Strangers have come into Egypt everywhere. . . . Men do not sail to Byblos today: What shall we do for fine wood? Princes and pious men everywhere as far as the land of Crete are em-balmed with the resins of Lebanon, but now we have no supplies. . . . The dead are thrown in the river. . . . Laughter has perished. Grief walks the land.[1]

[1] After Erman-Blackman: *Literature,* pp. 94–108.

This dismal picture is doubtless exaggerated, and in so far as it is true, must apply to the districts directly under the influence of the Residence near Memphis. Doubtless there were local governors who managed to keep some kind of order in their provinces, and in fact we have at least one stela from this period in which a magnate boasts that he made men, cattle, goats, asses, barley, and wheat to flourish by his own strong arm. But the cataclysm is plain for all to see. The art of the period is sparse and feeble, mostly a travesty of the Old Kingdom Memphite style. The materials are of poor quality, pottery, for instance largely replacing stone, faience, and metal in the manufacture of vessels. The internecine strife between one province and its neighbours is evident in the decoration of the model funerary boats with their cabin-roofs protected by large ox-hide shields. A ruler in Asyut was buried with two companies of model warriors to render service in some troubled after-life. Another nomarch of this same region boasts how the land was in terror before his soldiers, and how all were afraid when they beheld smoke arising in the South. Macabre reminders of the strife of these days are the bodies of some sixty shock-troops who were accorded honoured burial in a common tomb at Thebes. Their wounds showed that they had fallen in the desperate storming of some key-fortress.

Plate 21

With Egypt divided against itself, there was the inevitable immigration of foreigners into the rich pastures of the Delta. Famine in their own lands always drove Libyans and the wandering Semites of Sinai and the Negeb to graze their flocks on the borders of the Delta in the manner of Abraham and Jacob; and now with organized resistance removed, advantage was taken of this hospitality to add to the general tale of lawlessness and usurpation. The evils caused by social revolution, poverty, and anarchy brought others in their train such as famine, plague, and sterility. A deep traumatic impression was left on the Ancient Egyptian and made him only

Plate 17

too conscious that the greatest misfortune that could befall him was the removal of the divine authority of the Pharaoh. From that simple event all miseries seemed to flow.

The history of the First Intermediate Period is concerned with the painful attempts by successive strong men to restore the old peace and order. The most notable of these efforts was made by a powerful family living at Herakleopolis near the Faiyum who appear to have united all Middle Egypt under their sway and to have extended in time their influence over most of the Delta. Upper Egypt, however, from a little south of Abydos to the border at Elephantine, seems to have pre-served some kind of nominal independence under princes ruling at Thebes. The Herakleopolitans form Dynasties IX and X, and according to Manetho the founder of their line, Akhthoes, achieved supreme power 'by great cruelty which wrought woes for Egypt'. His name has survived on a number of small monuments; but there is a significant reference to a book of instruction in Statecraft which he wrote for his descendants, though it has not so far come to light. It must however be the forerunner of two such works which we shall shortly have to consider. After a century in which the Herakleo-politans appear to have consolidated their power by expelling the Asiatic squatters in the Delta, fortifying the eastern borders, re-establishing the importance of Memphis, improving irriga-tion works, and reopening trade with Byblos, the rising pretensions of the aggressive Thebans constituted a threat which could not be ignored, and sporadic fighting broke out between the rival powers with varying fortunes until the Theban prince Menthu-hotep I Neb-hepet-re decisively de-feated the Herakleopolitans and reunited Egypt under the rule of one Pharaoh.

The interludes between the great epochs of civilization in Egypt had their birth-pangs as well as their death-agonies. The prophet Ipuwer who deplored so loudly the change and

c. 2150–2058 B.C.

Plate 23

decay in all around him could not see its creative aspects though he himself was deeply involved in them. Out of the social revolution of the time, which cast aside the old accepted forms of expression, and out of the acute suffering, which moved men to cry out with a new voice, there was born a secular literature quite different from what had preceded it, a literature, moreover, which continued to inspire Egyptian writers for centuries afterwards and helped to sustain an accepted style. At a time when men were no longer ordered by the divine sanctions of Pharaonic authority, an appeal was made through the emotions by artistic processes; and the pessimistic literature that now flowered is cast in a poetic and elegant form. The ability of writing to influence men's minds is shrewdly recognized by a Herakleopolitan king who exhorts his son to be a craftsman in speech so that he might prevail, 'for power is in the tongue; and speech is mightier than fighting'.

Apart from *The Admonitions*, this literature contains *An Argument between a Man Contemplating Suicide and his Soul*, and *The Complaints of the Peasant*, a series of rather turgid but doubtless elegant speeches by an Egyptian 'character' who is humanely tormented for the sake of his eloquent protests. These writings appear to have emanated from the Court of the Herakleopolitans, and it is one of these kings, probably Wah⁄ka⁄re, who has left us another work in this group of Egyptian literary classics, *The Instruction for his Son, Mery⁄ka⁄re*. In this work, ideas appear which are different from the recipes for worldly success compiled by the Old Kingdom sages. There is, for instance, a confession of wrong⁄doing and repentance for past misdeeds. While much of the 'instruction' takes the form of practical advice from a ruler who has few illusions about the frailty and treachery of the human species, there is a distinct preoccupation with a code of conduct determined by abstract moral factors:

Do right as long as you are on earth. Calm the afflicted, oppress no widow, expel no man from his father's possessions. . . . Do not kill; but punish with beatings or imprisonment. Then shall this land be well established. Leave vengeance to God. . . . More acceptable to Him is the virtue of one who is upright of heart than the ox of the wrong-doer.[1]

While a new writing was thus being born out of suffering and its consequent mind-searching, the literary heritage of the Old Kingdom was undergoing a transformation directly connected with the social revolution. The promise of immortality in the Old Kingdom was greatly restricted; and it is doubtful whether in origin it extended beyond the divine king. He became a greater god upon death, and certain ceremonies were observed at his demise to make the transfiguration perfect; but what kind of after-life was enjoyed by his subjects is less clear—probably no more than a ghostly existence was thought to be the lot of his more privileged entourage, subsisting on the funerary offerings provided by their pious descendants. Around the tombs of the earliest dynastic kings were buried their servants, probably killed to accompany their masters in the hereafter; but substitutes were soon found for this savage custom, and in time the queens and members of the Royal family were naturally interred in tombs near the mastaba or pyramid of the king they had served in life and to whom they expected to stand in the same relationship after death. Such tombs and the immortality they assured were in the gift of the king; but when local governors began to make tombs in their own districts they inevitably took over something of the divine privileges of the Pharaoh himself. The history of burial customs thereafter, from the end of the Old Kingdom onwards, is the gradual arrogation by private

[1] After Erman-Blackman: *Literature*, p. 77.

persons of all the rights and appurtenances of Royal burial, and the process was greatly accelerated during the First Inter- mediate Period when so many minor lords regarded themselves as little inferior to kings. At the same time the general poverty made it necessary to find substitutes for all the lavish furnishings of the Royal burials. Thus instead of painted reliefs in fine limestone showing the procession of estates bringing their produce to the deceased, or the brewers, bakers, and butchers preparing the funerary meal, a few servant-statues, often crudely hacked out of wood, were provided to perform their offices by magic. Rectangular wooden coffins, decorated externally as though they were houses, were painted internally with pictures of equipment which had formerly been the exclusive trappings of Royalty—crowns, head-dresses, staves, sceptres, kilts, girdles, aprons, and tails. Even the uraeus-cobra, the essential symbol of Royalty, which the Pharaoh wore on his brow so that it might spit fire in the eyes of his enemies, was faithfully repre- sented. This wholesale usurpation did not stop at forms and emblems. The liturgy of the Royal burials was also taken over. At the end of Dynasty V and during Dynasty VI some chambers in the Royal pyramids were inscribed with magico- religious spells known to Egyptologists as *The Pyramid Texts*. These compilations were designed to perpetuate the prayers also daily offered by the funerary priests attached to the mortuary temple of the pyramid. They consist of random selections from a large corpus of utterances some of which, like the 'Cannibal Hymn', evidently date to Prehistoric times when the chieftain was a rain-maker, feasting ritually upon his slain enemies, and star-deities were worshipped. The majority of the spells, however, are concerned with the solar-cult of Heliopolis whose priests doubtless compiled *The Pyramid Texts*. When these writings were adopted by local princes, and their high officials, much of the liturgy was altered to make it suitable for use by private persons. New spells referring to

Plates 21, 22

contemporary conditions were added, and archaic utterances that could no longer be understood were omitted. In the impoverished burials of the period in which the offering-chamber is often very modest or non-existent, the practice arose of writing these texts in cursive hieroglyphs upon the interior of the coffins below the painted frieze of accoutrements, and the name of *The Coffin Texts* is given by Egyptologists to this new group of religious writings. The custom appears to have arisen in Herakleopolis and was continued throughout the ensuing Middle Kingdom for some Royal as well as private burials, although several of the more opulent tombs had their chapel-walls inscribed with the old Pyramid Texts, in this probably aping the Royal burials of Dynasty XII in which, however, funerary inscriptions have not survived.

It seems clear, therefore, that whatever impediments there were to achieving the supreme office of Pharaoh in life, few of the new governors and officials had any doubts about their becoming as kings at death.

2. THE MIDDLE KINGDOM

Dynasties XI–XIII, c. 2080–1640 B.C.

Throughout the Herakleopolitan period, the princes of Thebes had been able to exercise an uneasy suzerainty over the five southernmost districts of Upper Egypt, enclosing their names in cartouches like any Pharaoh. Their border with the Northern powers was at the city of Abydos, now coming into ever greater importance as the principal holy-seat of the god Osiris (see below, p. 116). In sporadic fighting this town changed hands several times and it was not until their prince, Menthu-hotep I Neb-hepet-re, came to power that the Thebans began to prevail over the loyalist powers. After several years of hard fighting, however, Menthu-hotep found himself the first effective Pharaoh of a united Egypt since the reign of Phiops II.

Plate 23

c. 2050 B.C.

Date B.C. and Years of Reign	Principal Kings	Main Sites	Funerary Customs	Significant Events
c. 2080	DYNASTY XI		*Coffin Texts* Large rock-	Reunion of Two
51	Menthu-hotep I Neb-hepet-re	Thebes	tomb with	Lands
12	Menthu-hotep II S-ankh-ka-re	Abydos	pyramid in forecourt	
c. 1990	DYNASTY XII			Development of
			Royal burials	Literature
30	Amun-em-het I (Ammenemes)	Thebes	in pyramids	Large irrigation
44	Sen-wosret I (Sesostris)	Lisht	Private burials	schemes in
18	Sen-wosret II	Dahshur	in mastabas	Faiyum. Re-
36	Sen-wosret III	Lahun	and rock-	building on all
50	Amun-em-het III	Hawara	tombs	sites. Final
				suppression of
c. 1785	DYNASTY XIII		Appearance	feudal nobles
			of anthropoid	Rise of Osiris-
	A large number of kings.		coffin and	cult at Abydos.
	Probably a separate line of		shawabti-	Subjugation of
	rulers in Western Delta		figure	Nubia. Trade
	forming Dynasty XIV			through Byblos
c. 1640				with Syria and
				Aegean

Table F   Middle Kingdom (Dynasties XI to XIII)

His gradual advance from a provincial kinglet to the 'Lord of
the Two Lands' is reflected in the funerary monument he
built at Deir el-Bahri with its early reliefs carved in a primly
rustic yet curiously attractive style, and the later work done
under the more sophisticated influence of Memphis. His
activities are recorded in many parts of the country, in the
region of the First Cataract, the Wadi Hammamat, and the
quarries of Hat-nub among other places, but he remained a
devotee of Southern culture making his Residence at Thebes

Plate 26
Fig. 37

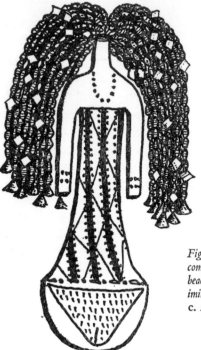

Fig. 35   Painted flat wooden doll with hair composed of strings of mud and faience beads, interwoven with squares of straw to imitate gold hair-rings; now at Edinburgh; c. 2000 B.C. Height 8½ in.

and building largely in Upper Egypt. There is more than a flavour of Nubian culture in his entourage, with his dark-skinned women-folk tattooed on their bodies, and in some of the artifacts, such as the curious 'paddle-dolls', that were buried with them. Menthu-hotep I celebrated a jubilee in his thirty-ninth regnal year and died after a long reign of fifty-one years during which he had a good opportunity of pacifying the land and guiding it back to some of its former prosperity. His eldest surviving son Menthu-hotep II S-ankh-ka-re inherited a united and tranquil State populated by a new generation to whom civil war was only a legend and devoted his short reign of twelve years to the arts of peace. A trading expedition was sent to Punt, a voyage which involved the conscription of an expeditionary force of three thousand men, the digging of wells and the cutting of stone in the Wadi Hammamat, the rounding‑up of hostile Bedouin *en route* and the building of a ship on the Red Sea coast for the transport of the myrrh‑resins from Somaliland. The blocks of cut stone were for the sanctuaries in temples which S‑ankh‑ka‑re built at Elephantine, Abydos, and hamlets near Thebes. Some of the reliefs with which they were adorned have survived and show that the refined carving and drawing characteristic of the last years of Neb‑hepet‑re continued to be followed, but with even greater skill and subtlety, and were not surpassed even by the sculptors of Dynasty XII, though they too worked in the same tradition, but with rather deeper relief.

cf. Fig. 40

Plate 24

As with the long reign of Phiops II, the fifty‑one years' rule of Menthu‑hotep I eventually created confusion in the dynastic succession and after the death of S‑ankh‑ka‑re, the country once more lapsed into anarchy. We catch a brief glimpse of a third Menthu‑hotep, and find that during his short reign another expedition, this time of ten thousand men under the command of the Vizier and Governor of the South, Amun‑em‑het, is in the Wadi Hammamat quarrying hard stone for the King's sarcophagus and its lid; then the mists of history come down again. When the scene clears, it is presumably the Vizier who is now on the throne ruling as Ammenemes I, the first Pharaoh of the powerful Dynasty XII.

c. 1990 B.C.

The new King found the wearing of the crowns of Upper and Lower Egypt an uneasy privilege. He was little more than the first among a number of jealous equals, such as the nomarchs of Hermopolis who arrogantly dated events to their own regnal years like any king; and the difficulties of his reign are sufficiently underlined by the co‑opting of his eldest son Sesostris to act as co‑regent in his twentieth regnal year and by his sudden death in his jubilee year. According to Manetho, Ammenemes was murdered by his own chamberlains, and there is further evidence for his violent end in a political testament, *The Teaching of King Ammenemes*, and in a novel, *The Story of Sinuhe*, which have survived as literary classics. The policies that he inaugurated, however, were carried out by his successors. While a Southerner, hailing from the Theban region to judge from his name, he abandoned the attempt to govern all Egypt from Thebes and moved his capital to the fulcrum of Upper and Lower Egypt some twenty miles south of Memphis near the modern el-Lisht. At the same time a determined attempt was made to subjugate Upper Nubia and the Sudan by the building of a string of fortified townships in the region all the way to Semna, and the planting of factories in the lands beyond, as at Kerma above the Third Cataract. The climax of this development was reached with Sesostris III who rebuilt most of the forts and was so intimately associated with the region that in after-years he was worshipped as the local god. While the Southern border was pushed farther upstream by a deliberate policy of expansion, the north-eastern frontier of Egypt which had so frequently been penetrated by Asiatics, was consolidated by means of a fortified barrier known as 'The Walls of the Prince', doubtless a series of strongholds set up at strategic points to command all the usual routes in and out of Egypt. During the last year of the co-regency, Sesostris I seems to have fought a campaign in Libya to repress raids on the western borders of the Delta.

Political activity to protect the frontiers is matched by greatly increased intercourse with Palestine and Syria, where objects bearing the names of different kings of Dynasties XII and XIII have been found at Gaza, Byblos, Ras Shamra, Megiddo, and elsewhere. *The Story of Sinuhe* (see below, p. 120) acquaints us with the fact that regular journeys by king's envoys were made to Syria by the beginning of the dynasty, and a deposit of Asiatic treasure in a temple near Thebes shows that the trade

Fig. 36   Three-handled jar of late Minoan Ib type found at Saqqara, c. 1480 B.C.; and a false-necked jar of late Helladic III type found at Gurob near Lahun; c. 1320 B.C. Scale, 1 : 3.

was not all in one direction. We also have a reference to a war against the Asiatics in the reign of Ammenemes I and a more ambitious campaign under Sesostris III, when Shechem was taken. Generally speaking, however, relations with Asia during this period seem to have been peaceful and largely concerned with trade. It was doubtless from Byblos or some such *entrepôt* that Aegean products reached Egypt and have left their trace in deposits of characteristic pottery at Abydos and elsewhere. Conversely, Egyptian objects of Middle Kingdom date have been excavated in Crete. The mining centres in Sinai also show evidence of the tremendous vigour with which the kings of this period increased the supplies of copper ores and turquoise from this source. The extent of all this foreign trade is but an index of the prosperity in Egypt itself. The capital at Lisht was near the Faiyum and the kings of Dynasty XII devoted a good deal of attention to land reclamation and hydraulic engineering in this region, turning it into one of the most fertile districts of Egypt. Sesostris I proved to be a most energetic builder, founding a great new temple at Heliopolis, where to commemorate his jubilee obelisks were erected, one of which still stands. He built or rebuilt on sites all over Egypt, not neglecting the family seat at Thebes whose obscure god,

Amun, now begins to come to the fore, as the name of several kings of the dynasty proudly proclaims. The Theban buildings of the Middle Kingdom were used as quarries by later Pharaohs and it is out of the foundations of the Third Pylon that there has recently been reconstructed a white limestone kiosk which Sesostris I built at Thebes for a symbolical re-enactment of his main jubilee ceremonies at Memphis.[1] The vitality shown by the architects of Sesostris I was shared in differing measure by their successors and reached its apogee during the reign of Ammenemes III for whom building and sculpture on a truly colossal scale was created. By that time, however, the Pharaoh had once more gained a lonely and unchallenged pre-eminence thanks to the policies pursued by his predecessors, particularly by his father Sesostris III who had evidently broken the power of the last of the feudal nobility and reduced them to the level of Crown officials. It is during his reign that the great series of provincial tombs at Beni Hasan and Deir el-Bersha come to a sudden end, as those at Asyut and Meir had ceased a generation earlier.

The fifty-year-long reign of Ammenemes III, the last great king of Dynasty XII, stored up troubles for the succession soon after, and the following dynasty ruled for a confused century during which we have scant details of too many kings to suggest that it was either prosperous or tranquil. The capital remained at Lisht despite the Theban names of many of these rulers. At times some kind of control seems to have been exercised by more vigorous kings or co-regents; also building operations went on at the old centres, and trade continued with Byblos, but a steady decline in artistic and technical standards, and a gradual poverty in ideas and materials tell their own story. A significant portent is the appearance of several Asiatic names in the king-lists of this dynasty, and under a certain Dudumose an event occurred which

[1] H. Kees: *Mitteilungen d. Deutschen Archäol. Inst. Kairo*, 16, pp. 194–213.

Plate 25

Plate 33

receives special mention by Josephus who quotes Manetho at length:

> Tutimaeus. In his reign, for what cause I know not, a blast of God smote us; and unexpectedly, from the regions of the East, invaders of obscure race marched in confidence of victory against our land. By main force they easily seized it without striking a blow; and having overpowered the rulers of the land, they then burned our cities ruthlessly, razed to the ground the temples of the gods, and treated all the natives with a cruel hostility. . . .[1]

Thus ended ingloriously, according to the official accounts, ✓ the second great period in the history of Egyptian culture destroyed by the Hyksos invasion (see however p. 123 below).

c. 1640 B.C.

While the nomarchs of the First Intermediate Period had taken over most of the style and ritual of Royal burial, they were still interred in rock-cut tombs, a practice which continued for wealthy private burials with a few exceptions throughout the Middle Kingdom. The princes of Thebes followed the general custom in having tombs hewn in the western hills opposite Karnak with large courtyards levelled in front of them. Menthu-hotep I had begun such a tomb laid out on a generous scale in a huge bay among the cliffs at Deir el-Bahri, but it underwent several changes of plan, perhaps with the growing ambitions of the King, and in its final form was a synthesis of the Theban portico-tombs of his ancestors and the traditional pyramids of Old Kingdom Pharaohs. Its unknown architect showed a remarkable eye for the picturesque exploitation of a site with his use of terraces and colonnades. A curious feature of the monument was a dummy tomb in its courtyard with a burial chamber under the pyramid containing a statue of the King in jubilee costume wrapped in linen like a mummy. This statue with its flesh painted black, the crown red, and the jubilee-cloak white is

Plate 23

[1] W. G. Waddell: *Manetho*, p. 79.

well calculated to give a savage force to what has been regarded as a substitute for the ceremonially killed corpse of the divine king. It may be, however, that Menthu-hotep provided two tombs for himself on the same site; a rock-hewn tomb for his corpse as King of Upper Egypt, and a pyramid-tomb for a statue of himself as King of Lower Egypt wearing the Red Crown. In the precincts and vicinity of this temple were cut the rock-tombs of several relatives and officials, including the pit-tombs and adjacent shrines of six of the royal women, some of whose funerary equipment has survived, while that of Menthu-hotep himself has been robbed and destroyed. Also near at hand was the famous chapel of his half-sister, Queen Neferu, with its painted limestone reliefs, and the walls of the burial chamber decorated with offerings, friezes of objects, and versions of *The Coffin Texts*, like the interior of a huge contemporary coffin (see above, p. 107).

With the transfer of the capital from Thebes to the North in Dynasty XII, there came a return to the Lower Egyptian form of Royal tomb, particularly under Sesostris I who erected a pyramid at Lisht which shows the direct inspiration of the funerary monument of Phiops II, not only in its size, plan, and scheme of decoration but in the very style of the reliefs. The kings of Dynasty XII also renewed the old practice of building the mastaba-tombs of their high officials and mortuary priests around their own pyramids but on a very reduced scale, for the truth now was that burial near the king had become something of an anachronism with the rise to importance of the cult of the god Osiris. In origin this god may have been a corn-deity introduced from Asia with cereal crops in Prehistoric times. Very early in his career he was assimilated to an old deified pastoral chieftain of Djedu in the Eastern Delta which became one of his holy cities. By Dynasty V, however, he had begun to absorb the funerary god of Abydos in Upper Egypt which eventually achieved prominence as his chief cult-centre.

Plate 26

Plate 34

Fig. 6

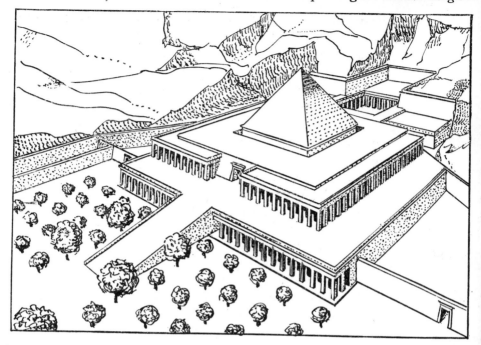

37   *Reconstruction of the funerary temple of Menthu-hotep I at Deir el-Bahri, Western Thebes. In the court-yard was planted a grove of tamarisks with eight larger sycamore-figs shading statues of the King; c. 2011 B.C.*

With the increase in the power of the Theban dynasty in the later years of the First Intermediate Period and their capture of Abydos, the claims of Osiris were greatly extended. From being a minor god of agriculture and of the Nile who was identified with the dead king in *The Pyramid Texts*, Osiris in the Middle Kingdom became the god of the dead *par excellence* and every deceased person who in hopes of immortality had usurped all the trappings and prerogatives of Royal burial was represented as the dead king, Osiris, even adopting the epithet of 'The Osiris (so-and-so)'. The increase in the pretensions of Abydos is seen in the great wealth of remains there, dating from the Early Middle Kingdom onwards, from the hundreds

cf. Plates 20, 58

117

of round-topped stelae and votive statues of private persons to the cenotaph of Sesostris III, all anxious to have some station near the 'staircase of the Great God', even if burial in the holy ground itself was not possible. While the cult of Osiris was concerned entirely with the life after death, and did not challenge that of other deities, a certain amount of encroachment was inevitable as Osiris took over the judicial powers which the sun-god Re, for instance, had exercised over the Heliopolitan tribunal, and became the supreme judge of the dead, before whom all wandering souls after death had to account for their deeds on earth. The prestige of the Pharaoh as a divinity, already sadly eroded from the last years of the Old Kingdom, suffered further decay with the ascendancy of Osiris as the deification of the idea of kingship. From now on, all men who were worthy had the promise of immortality in the realms ruled over by the kingly divinity Osiris, not merely those who had known the Pharaoh in life. There was of course no revolutionary cleavage of thought since the Pharaoh, on death, was assimilated to Osiris.

The decline which this religious development and the new political circumstances wrought in the kingship during the First Intermediate Period was arrested and reversed during Dynasty XII when a series of remarkable literary works were written in praise of various kings. Some scholars, notably the Frenchman Posener, have interpreted these writings very plausibly as deliberate attempts at propaganda on behalf of the divine supremacy of the Pharaoh. The first of them is a sort of *post-hoc* prophecy, known to Egyptologists as *The Prophecy of Neferti*, and describes how in the spacious days of King Sneferu of Dynasty IV a great prophet, Neferti, is called to the Court to divert the King with 'choice speeches'. He describes what is to happen in the land in the distant future, using phrases which recall those of *The Admonitions* (see p. 102) of an earlier date:

I show thee the land wailing and weeping . . . a man's spirit will be concerned with his own welfare. . . . Every mouth is full of, 'Pity me!' All good things have departed. The land is destroyed.

The Prophecy, however, ends on a more cheerful note:

A king shall come forth from Upper Egypt called Ameni, the son of a woman of the South. . . . He shall receive the White Crown and wear the Red Crown. . . . Be glad, ye people of his time! The son of a high-born man will make his name for all eternity. They who would make mischief and devise enmity have suppressed their mutterings through fear of him. . . . There shall be built the 'Walls of the Prince' and the Asiatics shall not again be suffered to go down to Egypt. They shall beg again for water for their cattle after their custom. . . . And Right [*Ma'at*] shall come into its own again and Wrong shall be cast out.[1]

The Ameni of the prophecy is undoubtedly Ammenemes I, and his Upper Egyptian parentage, which was noble, is stressed as an apologia for his seizure of supreme power to end the miseries of anarchy at the close of Dynasty XI.

The second work, *The Teaching of King Ammenemes*, already mentioned, is concerned with events at the end of the reign of the same King, who was apparently murdered or ritually killed by his chamberlains. In *The Teaching* the dead King is made to appear in a dream to his son Sesostris I in order to give him some sage advice in the manner of the earlier *Instructions for King Mery-ka-re* (see above, p. 105):

Be on thy guard against subordinates. . . . Trust not a brother, know not a friend and make not for thyself intimates. . . .

[1] After Erman-Blackman: *Literature*, pp. 110-15.

But *The Teaching* then goes on to justify this scepticism on the strength of the experiences of the King himself who had received nothing but ingratitude from those he had promoted. The major part of the work is, in fact, not a 'teaching' at all, but a second apologia for the King's life and eulogy of his achievements. It could also be in the nature of an official explanation and excuse for any extreme measures that the young co-regent may have had to take on the sudden and violent death of his father.

The third of these works of propaganda, *The Story of Sinuhe*, is cast in a typically Egyptian literary form, the novel, and is a simple success-story told with an elegance, dramatic concise-ness, and humour that we can still appreciate. The scene opens in the camp of the young co-regent Sesostris I who is returning from a successful campaign in Libya when the news of his father's death is brought to him. With a few picked followers the King leaves hurriedly for the Residence without informing the Army; but Sinuhe, an official in the service of the Queen, overhears the dire report, and flees from the camp in panic, so beginning his odyssey. Scholars have been wont to interpret this flight as a confession of Sinuhe's complicity in some palace intrigue, but that is largely because they regard the story as faithfully reflecting historical events instead of being pure romance. The justification that Sinuhe gives for his behaviour is quite explicit and is the motive of the plot: 'It was', he says, 'like the dispensation of God . . . after the manner of a dream', and it is as a god-struck man that he continues his wanderings. Fate takes him thus to the Lebanon where he is received by a local prince, Amunenshi, who gives him his eldest daughter in marriage and grants him lands on his borders. Here Sinuhe spends many years while his children grow up to be chieftains of their tribes. He acts as the commander of Amunenshi's forces and greatly increases his territories, defeating in single combat a Goliath-like champion among the Asiatics. He had not, however, entirely lost contact with Egypt and entertained the King's messengers on their lawful occasions. They reported to Sesostris the ageing exile's heart-felt prayer to return to the land of his birth and to the service of his mistress the Queen. The King graciously invites Sinuhe to return to Court and the triumphant rehabilitation of Sinuhe, like the Prodigal Son, concludes the novel.

The Story of Sinuhe is remarkable for the semblance of actuality that is given to all the incidents in the tale, suggesting a real tomb-autobiography rather than a work of the imagination. Apart from the divine impulsion that sets Sinuhe on his wanderings, the tale is free from the supernatural interventions of later Egyptian stories. Although the setting is fairyland—to the Court Egyptian of Dynasty XII, Asia was *terra incognita* where everything was possible—all the dramatis personae behave in a completely rational manner. But there are two heroes of the story, the protagonist Sinuhe and Sesostris I, himself, who remains prominent in the background, from the opening paragraphs dealing with his victorious return from war, through the apostrophes to him in the body of the work, and the elegant letter inviting Sinuhe to return, to his kindly reception of the fugitive and the honours he heaps upon him. Sesostris is shown first as the dutiful son and valiant warrior conquering through love as much as might, and finally as the god-like ruler, forgiving and generous.

These and other minor works, hymns in praise of the kings and so forth, form the classical literature of Egypt, and helped to enhance the prestige of the Pharaoh during the Middle Kingdom. They were painfully learnt by schoolboys even half a millennium later, and quotations from them are to be found unexpectedly in solemn monumental inscriptions during the New Kingdom. That the kings of Dynasty XII should enlist the services of skilful writers to sustain their power and glamour may at first seem startling, and probably it was no explicit

Fig. 48

Plates 23,
29–31, 33

directive that brought such literature into being, but the plastic
arts reveal the same subconscious desire to show the King as
a superman. The Royal statues of this reign are remarkable for
their forceful portrayal of the King either as the ruthless or
regal overlord of the nation, or later as the world-weary 'Good
Shepherd' of his people. Most of this sculpture in hard stones,
such as obsidian, granites, quartzites, and basalts, is of magnificent workmanship, both technically and artistically, with a
haunting inner power.

Plate 32

While Royal statuary is differentiated by individual portraiture, private sculpture merely follows the fashion of a
particular reign. Much of it was shop-work and on a small
scale made for sale to modest patrons like the pilgrims to
Abydos, and varies from the competent to the frankly inept.
The chasm between the superb creations of the Court sculptors
and this mediocre hack-work only emphasizes the gulf between
the King, aloof at the head of affairs, and the mass of the people
which had been opened again by the end of Dynasty XII.
At the same time, the great number of votive stelae and statues
suggests that the little man had increased his prosperity at the
expense of the great feudal lords.

CHAPTER VII

The Second Breakdown and Recovery during the New Kingdom

I. THE SECOND INTERMEDIATE PERIOD

Dynasties XIV–XVII, c. 1640–1570 B.C.

IN THE PAST, scholars have been inclined to accept Manetho's account of the appearance of the Hyksos in Egypt as the sudden irruption of a conquering horde spreading fire and destruction everywhere. In recent years, a reconsideration of the material has led to rather different conclusions. In the first place, no precise archaeological evidence for the Hyksos as an invading force has been uncovered in the deposits of the period, and pottery and fortifications which were once believed to be their work are now thought to have different origins.

If the conquerors arrived therefore as aliens, either they must have had a material culture which was identical with that of their Egyptian hosts, or they very quickly and completely adopted local manners and customs on arrival. Manetho by a false etymology translated the word *Hyksos* as 'Shepherd Kings', whereas 'Rulers of Uplands' would have been more accurate. Under this title, such people are well known in the Egypt of the Middle Kingdom, a group of them being represented for instance in their 'coats of many colours' in a tomb at Beni Hasan. These Rulers of Uplands were no more than wandering Semites trading their products with Egypt, or going down there for sanctuary, or to buy corn, or water their flocks according to an age-old tradition. The story of Joseph reveals how some of these Asiatics may have arrived, sold into serfdom for corn in time of famine, or offering themselves as menials in return for food and shelter. Recent study of a papyrus in the

Plate 35

cf. Plate 17

Brooklyn Museum and other documents has revealed that numerous Asiatics were in Egypt, perhaps from the time of the First Intermediate Period, acting as cooks, brewers, seamstresses, and the like. The children of these immigrants often took Egyptian names and so fade from our sight. Asiatic

dancers and a doorkeeper in a temple of Sesostris II are known, showing that these foreigners attained positions of importance and trust. It is not difficult to see that by the middle of Dynasty XIII, the lively and industrious Semites could be in the same positions of responsibility in the Egyptian State as Greek freedmen were to enjoy in the Government of Imperial Rome. Famine or ethnic movements leading to largescale infiltrations into the Delta of Semites, mixed perhaps with Hurrian elements, especially during the anarchy into which the Middle Kingdom lapsed, could have resulted in the founding of a Lower Egyptian State with an Asiatic king and officials taking over imperceptibly all the functions and machinery of Pharaonic government.

This in fact seems to have happened. A Hyksos principality was established on the eastern borders of the Delta with Avaris as its capital, whence Asiatic influence spread over Lower Egypt until Memphis itself was wrested almost without a blow from the tired hands of the last feeble ruler of Dynasty XIII. The Hyksos kings of whom we have names, and who are thought to have formed Dynasties XV and XVI, seem to have adopted Egyptian titularies, costume, and habits, writing their outlandish personal names, such as JacobEl, Anathher, and Khyan in hieroglyphs, and adopting Egyptian thronenames. They dutifully worshipped Re of Heliopolis, as well as Seth or Sutekh, the Egyptian equivalent of their Baal. That they were regarded as legitimate sovereigns in Lower Egypt at least is clear from their inclusion in the Turin kinglist written in Ramesside times, and on other documents.

By the seventeenth century B.C. the following political

situation seems to have been established in the Nile Valley: Lower Egypt was ruled by a line of Hyksos kings, probably with the help of Asiatic officials, inheriting all the prestige and responsibilities of the Egyptian Pharaoh, and exerting an influence beyond the Delta over territories in Sinai and Palestine. Upper Egypt, from Elephantine to Cusae north of Asyut, enjoyed an uneasy independence under its princes ruling at Thebes by paying tribute to the Hyksos overlord. From Elephantine southwards, Nubia and the Lower Sudan were also independent under a separate Prince of Kush, but in alliance with the Hyksos, and this extraordinary state of affairs requires some explanation.

The Pharaohs of the Middle Kingdom had subjugated the Sudan as far as the Second Cataract and had established factories beyond this frontier at least as far as Kerma. Here a curious hybrid culture flourished, employing Egyptian techniques in faience and metal, yet also using such alien materials as mica and shell, and native-inspired designs. As early as the reign of Ammenemes II, the Count Hapdjefi, the governor of this region, who had prepared a handsome tomb and endowment for himself in his native Asyut, was buried at Kerma under a large tumulus surrounded by his servants and women-folk. These had been drugged and suffocated to accompany their master in the other world, and if Hapdjefi could so far forget all the instincts of the civilized Egyptian as to accept the local barbaric custom of sati-burial, assuming he had a choice in the matter, it would be small wonder if in the course of a few generations hereditary governors should not have gone entirely native and sought to assert an independence in the face of the crumbling metropolitan power in distant Egypt, as was to happen in similar circumstances in the eleventh century B.C. The formidable fortresses built during Dynasty XII between the First and Second Cataracts were all stormed and destroyed during the Second Intermediate Period, a task

c. 1920 B.C.

Plate 37

surely beyond the skill of a primitive though warlike folk, unless they were directed by officers versed in the military operations of a civilized State.

While to Manetho the Hyksos seizure of supreme power seemed an unmitigated disaster, we can recognize it as one of the great fertilizing influences in Egyptian civilization, bringing fresh blood, new ideas, and different techniques into the Valley and ensuring that Egypt kept to the mainstream of the Bronze Age culture in the Eastern Mediterranean. A number of innovations now appear. Even during the time of the Asiatic invasions of the Delta at the end of the Old Kingdom, a curious perforated hemispherical seal, known to archaeologists as a button-seal, made its appearance. During the Middle Kingdom this was transformed into the characteristic Egyptian scarab, perhaps more of an amulet than a seal, and this artifact was adopted with enthusiasm by the Hyksos who produced them in enormous numbers. With the Hyksos, too, bronze comes into general use. It was easier to work than copper and more effective for weapons and hardware generally. In the later phases of the war of liberation that developed between the Hyksos and the Thebans at the end of our period, a whole range of novel weapons was introduced from Asia, such as the horse-drawn chariot, scale armour, the composite bow, and new designs of daggers, swords, and scimitars. It is doubtful whether such weapons as the horse and chariot were fully effective in Egypt where the inundation and the topography gave a greater importance to water-borne operations; but the Thebans certainly adopted all these weapons in their wars against the Hyksos both in Egypt and Palestine. The Asiatic origin of the chariot was preserved in the different woods used in its construction, the Canaanite names for its

Fig. 38   Group of button, scarab and cylinder-seals in glazed steatite inscribed with the names of kings and private persons and with meander patterns; c. 2100 and 1780 B.C. Scale, 2 : 3

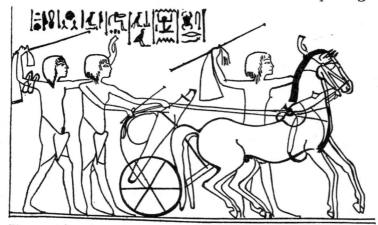

Fig. 39 A horse-drawn chariot waiting while grooms applaud the decoration of their master, the Chief of Police, by the Pharaoh; outline drawing in ink in the tomb of Mahu at Amarna; c. 1360 B.C. Scale 1 : 10.

various parts, and by the tradition of retaining Asiatics to drive and maintain some of them at least. A war-helmet, probably made of leather sewn with gilded metal disks, was added to the Pharaoh's regalia and is known to Egyptologists as the Blue, or War Crown.

Plates 42, 55

More important than these weapons of destruction were certain abiding inventions of peace, such as improved methods of spinning and weaving, using an upright loom; new musical instruments, a lyre, the long-necked lute, the oboe, and tambourine. Hump-backed bulls were imported from an Asiatic source, probably brought by ship with the greatly increased trade that the Hyksos fostered. Other importations included the olive and pomegranate tree.

In Thebes during this period, the poverty and lack of good timber encouraged further changes in funerary customs and the self-contained burial comes into fashion. There had indeed been a shift of emphasis during the last quarter of Dynasty XII when a new expression creeps into the funerary prayers to indicate that the deceased was regarded less as a materialization than as a spirit. At the same time, under the impact of the Osiris-cult, the coffin as a sort of rectangular wooden house is replaced by the anthropomorphic case decorated to represent the deceased as the mummified and resurrected Osiris.

With the appearance of this type of coffin, the tomb-statue, already greatly reduced, either disappears or is transformed into the funerary statuette or shawabti (later ushabti) figure. Such objects do not make their appearance before Dynasty XI and the first examples are in wax, but by the end of the Middle Kingdom they were being made of stone or the wood of the persea (*shawab*) tree, and inscribed with the full shawabti chapter from the so-called *Book of the Dead*, a collection of funerary prayers and spells written on linen shrouds and later on papyrus rolls which replaced *The Coffin Texts* as the rectangular sarcophagi were discarded. The shawabti-figure was a specialized form of the servant-statue which had disappeared with the triumph of the Osiris faith. Its purpose was to act as a substitute for the deceased whenever onerous toil had to be performed in the fields of the Osirian other-world. In Egypt from the earliest times a *corvée* had existed whereby labourers could be drafted *en masse* for public works at critical moments during the inundation. Similar duties were naturally expected in the agricultural realms of Osiris, and it was to exempt the deceased from such forced labour that the shawabti was provided. By the end of this period even the king, who on death was assimilated to Osiris, was thought to be subject to this same conscription, and royal shawabtis are many and elaborate.

Plate 63

The lack of good timber as well as changes in doctrine hastened the disappearance of the rectangular outer coffin and the sole anthropoid containers were now dug out of local fig-trees and are invariably ill-shaped and crude. They were painted with a characteristic feathered decoration representing the wings of the sky-mother, Nut, who according to a pastiche of several brief spells from *The Pyramid Texts* regularly found on the coffin-lids of the next dynasty, is exhorted to extend herself over the deceased so that he might not die but be placed among the Imperishable Stars which were in her.

THE NEW KINGDOM

Dynasties XVIII–XX, c. 1570–1075 B.C.

About the year 1600 B.C. a certain Teti-sheri ('little Teti'), the daughter of a commoner, was married to the Prince of Thebes who recognized the overlordship of the Hyksos king in Avaris. By the time she died as a little, white-haired, partially bald, old woman, her grandson was the Pharaoh of a united Egypt and the most powerful prince of the age. This dramatic rise from rags to riches was not achieved without a bitter struggle. A novelette of later years relates how her son Seken-en-re fought a diplomatic battle of words with the Hyksos overlord Apophis, and although the end of the tale is missing we are to assume that the verbal victory lay with the Theban. This is apparently the same Seken-en-re who was less successful on a more strenuous battlefield for he met a violent end (see p. 63 above). But the last word was not with Apophis. Seken-en-re's elder son, Kamose, began a war of liberation in earnest, and we are fortunate in having his account of the opening of the campaign on two stelae, the second of which came to light only in 1954 among some foundation-blocks at Thebes. We learn that the young King sailed downstream with his forces and stormed the stronghold of a collaborator, Teti, near Hermopolis, pushing his boundary to within some twenty leagues of the Faiyum. In this campaign he succeeded in capturing a Hyksos treasure-fleet, and in intercepting a messenger who had been sent by Apophis with a letter to his ally, the Prince of Kush, exhorting him to fall upon Kamose in the rear.

Date B.C. and Years of Reign	Principal Rulers	Funerary Customs	Foreign Affairs	Significant Events
1570	DYNASTY XVIII		Nubia and Kush under Egyptian Viceroy	Introduction of bronze and new weapons, horse and chariot
25	Ahmosis		New dependencies in Palestine	
21	Amun-hotep (Amenophis I)		and Syria	
19	Tuthmosis I	Kings buried	Diplomatic	Glass-working
21	Q. Hatshepsut	in elaborate	relations with	Trade with Punt
54	Tuthmosis III	rock-tombs	Cyprus, Aegean,	restored
25	Amenophis II	at Thebes:	Anatolia,	
14	Tuthmosis IV	separate mortuary	Babylon	
39	Amenophis III	temples	*Fall of Knossos*	
17	Amenophis IV (Akhenaten)	Private burials in rock-tombs	Loss of influence in Asia	Akhenaten's failure to
9	Tut-ankh-amun	at Thebes and	Rise of Hittites	impose mono-
?	Haremhab	elsewhere gradually		theism Appearance of
1304	DYNASTY XIX	become less opulent: ten-	Attempt to challenge	iron weapons
13	Sethos I	dency for	Hittites in	Capital moved
67	Ramesses II	self-contained	Syria. Treaty	from Thebes to
12	Merenptah	burial in highly decorated	between Egypt and Hittites	Pi-Ramesse Great building
1181	DYNASTY XX	coffin. Magic funerary texts written on	*Fall of Troy*	activity Army recruits mercenaries
2	Set-nakht	papyrus rolls	Ethnic move-	Decline in
32	Ramesses III and eight other Ramessides	(*The Book of the Dead*)	ments in Mediterranean Eclipse of Hittites Repulse of Libyans and Sea-Peoples Loss of Asiatic	prestige of king- ship Tomb robberies at Thebes Rebellion in Middle Egypt
1075			dependencies	

Table G New Kingdom (Dynasties XVIII to XX)

Neither Kamose nor Apophis lived to see the end of the affair and it was left to Ahmosis, the former's younger brother, to carry on the struggle, eventually reducing the Hittite capital, Avaris, after a long siege. To consolidate his gains he had to fight a series of campaigns not only against the Hyksos in Palestine where their base at Sharuhen was destroyed, but also against their collaborators within Egypt, and their Kushite allies. While Ahmosis was regarded by the Egyptians as the first king of Dynasty XVIII and the founder of a new and glorious era in Egyptian history, it is now evident that his account of his victories is somewhat tendentious. The Hyksos are dismissed as foreigners and the several native loyalists as rebels, and it must have been the official narrative of the triumphant Thebans that Manetho drew upon for his picture of the Hyksos as a horde of infidel oppressors. Ahmosis also fought a campaign in Phoenicia and this violent irruption into the affairs of Palestine and Syria was continued by his successors, particularly by the great warrior-king Tuthmosis III who firmly extended Egyptian influence to the Euphrates.

Plate 36

c. 1469 B.C.

By committing Egypt to aggressive intervention in Asia, a pattern was set which persisted for centuries. In these military enterprises the advantage was heavily on the side of the Egyptians who possessed an army, battle-trained, with a high morale, and imbued for the first time in history with a nationalistic fervour. Moreover, the Egyptians were always ready to take the field just when the Asiatics were about to gather their crops. Their Syrian and Canaanite opponents were loose federations of different Powers lacking all cohesion. In Palestine, Lebanon, and Syria the political unit was the city-state ruling over the territories in the vicinity of its walls and receiving into its sanctuary the local populace in times of trouble. These States, like their equivalents in Renaissance Italy, were in constant rivalry with each other. Occasionally, under the leadership of a prince more energetic and crafty than his fellows, a coalition of States would win some stability, but too great a success would engender its own reaction and the federation would dissolve and re-form in another direction.

While these various States hardly welcomed the interference of a Big Brother, they were only too ready to turn intervention to their own advantage, following the Power whose star was in the ascendant and seeking its assistance in promoting their own local ambitions. But sometimes it was doubtful to whom fortune would incline the supremacy, and in such cases one big Power was played off against the other, vows of loyalty given to both, and sides changed and re-changed with little compunction. This is the world of Palestine and Syria that has been revealed to us from the Amarna diplomatic correspondence, which also apprises us of the intrusions of a mysterious people known as the Sa-Gaz or Khabiru, whom some scholars regard as the Hebrews. The Khabiru appear to have been displaced persons of both sexes moving around like robber-bands and probably keeping to difficult country away from the military high-roads, and intervening in the local politics by accepting service as mercenaries when they were not fighting on their own account.

The initial Egyptian forays into Western Asia made their impression on the local rulers who hastened to show their
Plate 41
submission by sending tribute, but by the time Tuthmosis III attained to sole rule much of this goodwill had leaked away thanks to the influence of the rising new Power of Mitanni. The Mitanni were mostly Hurrians, ruled by an Aryan aristocracy who worshipped Indo-European gods, and inhabited the watershed of the Euphrates. On the east they were bounded by the young nation of Assyria and on the west by the Hittites, a mixed people occupying most of Anatolia, with an Indo-European ruling class speaking a language akin to Greek and Latin. At the beginning of our

period Mitanni was the dominant Power in North Syria, having conquered the eastern Hittite territories.

Tuthmosis III found it necessary to fight seventeen cam-paigns over a period of some twenty years before his claims in Palestine and Syria could be recognized and the pretensions of Mitanni checked. In the course of these wars Egypt was forced to organize her Asiatic sphere of influence into a virtual dependancy, forming garrison-towns at strategic points and removing the sons of local rulers to Egypt as hostages for their fathers' good behaviour. These sons were brought up with the Egyptian Royal children 'to serve their lord and stand at the portal of the king'. Eventually they went back to rule their States after having been anointed by the Pharaoh himself. Peaceful relations, too, were soon entertained with Mitanni, an alliance which was cemented by the marriages of the Pharaohs to Mitannian princesses.

c. 1489– 1469 B.C.

By 1370 B.C., however, under the able king Suppiluliumas, the fortunes of the Hittites greatly revived and they intervened vigorously in affairs on their southern and eastern borders. The Mitannian capital was sacked and its king subsequently assassinated. Syria came under the dominance of the Hittites who fostered intrigue and dissension farther south by means of their agents. At this moment, Egypt, the ally of Mitanni, issued no effective challenge to the Hittite threat, her government being in the hands of the eccentric Akhenaten whose attention was largely devoted to affairs in his own remote capital. Egyptian influence in Syrian politics thereafter declined steeply and it is doubtful whether the remaining Pharaohs of Dynasty XVIII were able to do much to restore it. The power-ful kingdom of Mitanni riven by civil strife became a mere satellite of the Hittites and was eventually incorporated into the expanding State of Assyria on the death of Suppiluliumas, and disappears from history.

Plate 46

While events in Asia followed a fluctuating course, the

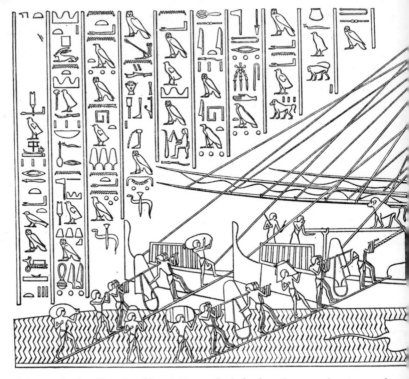

Fig. 40   Loading Egyptian ships at Punt with the local products, myrrh-resin, myrrh-tree of Hatshepsut at Deir el-Bahri, Western Thebes; c. 1478 B.C. Scale, 1 : 9.

Fig. 47

more important Southern dependencies of Nubia and Kush, the Biblical 'Ethiopia', came under effective Egyptian government as never before. The early kings of Dynasty XVIII had campaigned regularly in these regions and extended the southernmost frontier to Napata near modern Gebel Barkal. The entire territory was now put in charge of a high official or viceroy, called 'the King's Son of Kush', appointed by the Pharaoh and responsible to him alone. Under a peaceful and efficient rule, the region prospered; irrigation-works improved the fertility of the soil; new cities were founded and at least a

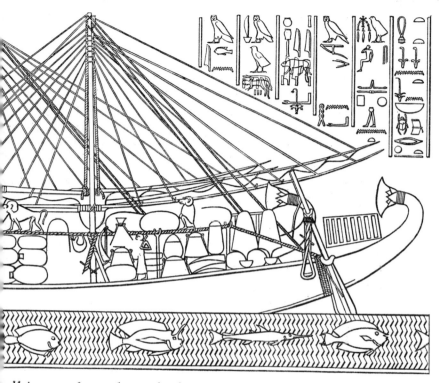

gold, incense-woods, apes, dogs, panther-skins, natives and their children; from a relief in the temple

dozen new temples built, some of them of great size, such as the one erected by Amenophis III at Soleb. The Egyptianization of Nubia and Kush was so effective that at the end of the New Kingdom, the Viceroy intervened decisively in the affairs of Egypt proper in the name of law and order. The products of Nubia and Kush added greatly to the wealth of Egypt, particularly its gold, ivory, ebony, cattle, gums, and semi-precious stones.

Most of these same commodities were also obtained by trading ventures to Punt, always an indication of the health and vigour of the Egyptian State, and during this period such voyages become common-place. The first of these expeditions during Dynasty XVIII, in the reign of Queen Hatshepsut, is the most noteworthy for the detailed representation of it carved in relief on the Queen's funerary temple at Deir el-Bahri. Here we see the flotilla of five large ships sailing from their Red Sea port, the arrival at Punt where the inhabitants lived in grass huts built on piles, the Egyptians offering the trade-goods of all such African adventurers ever since—strings of beads, axes, and weapons—and the triumphant return with gold, ivory, apes, and precious myrrh-trees, their root-balls carefully protected by baskets for transplanting in Thebes.

The advent of Dynasty XIX brought a new dynamic into the affairs of Western Asia, and in the first year of his reign Sethos I set forth to follow the sacrosanct patterns of the campaigns of Tuthmosis III and win back the Syrian dominions. While Sethos was successful in re-establishing Egyptian authority in Canaan and in capturing the key-fortress of Kadesh on the Orontes, his battle with the Hittites was inconclusive; and it was left to his impetuous son Ramesses II to try conclusions with the prime enemy. In the latter's fifth regnal year the Egyptian forces fell into a trap set by the wily Hittite King north of Kadesh and were extricated from disaster only by the chance arrival of one of their army corps and by the personal valour of Ramesses in persistently charging the enemy in order to rally his demoralized forces. Thereafter no serious challenge was made to Hittite ascendancy in Northern Syria. The two Powers in fact entered into increasingly friendly relations culminating in a defensive alliance between them which is an important landmark in the history of diplomacy. In the treaty, of which a Hittite copy as well as Egyptian versions of the original inscribed silver tablet exist, both Powers act as equals; their spheres of influence are carefully defined, South Syria going to Egypt and the North to the

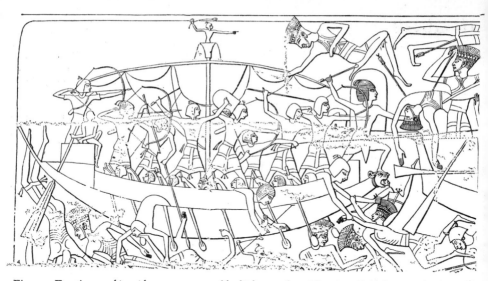

Fig. 41   Egyptian warship with oarsmen protected by high gunwales, soldiers in padded helmets, and a slinger in a crows-nest engage a Philistine boat in the combined fleet of the Sea-Peoples; from a relief in the temple of Ramesses III at Medinet Habu, Western Thebes; c. 1170 B.C. Scale, 1 : 20

Hittites; each pledges the other not to support its enemies, and there are provisions for the extradition of criminals or *emigrés*.

It may be that both Powers realized the futility of warring against each other in the face of a common menace. Neither side could foresee that both were on the threshold of a new age which was to change decisively the pattern of culture in the Mediterranean and bring the Classical world into being. The cause of the great migrations of peoples that now developed momentum seems to have been the pressure of populations from the Balkans and Black Sea areas upon the pre-Greek inhabitants of the islands and coasts of the Mediterranean. Soon after 1400 B.C. the Minoan Empire in Crete had been overwhelmed by Achaeans from the mainland, and piratical adventurers from these and related Sea-peoples now reached the African coast and allied themselves with the native Berber tribes. Increasing aridity in the region may have added to the unrest, and each generation of Egyptians during the next century had to face a determined attempt by a coalition of Libyans and Sea-peoples to occupy the rich lands of the Western Delta. A foray in the reign of Sethos I was easily repelled; but a much more formidable threat developed in the reign of his grandson, Merenptah, and the invaders were routed only after hard fighting. This heavy defeat gave Egypt nearly half a century of peace, disturbed by sporadic Libyan raids, during which her morale was sapped by the inevitable dynastic squabbles that arose after the long reign of Ramesses II. Ramesses III, however, the first great King of Dynasty XX and the last great Pharaoh of Egypt, had to repulse with great slaughter two desperate invasions from Libya led by the Meshwesh, the Classical Maxyes, and supported by such allies as the Philistines and Teucrians, and accompanied by their familes, cattle, and household goods. Even these disasters did not deter these land-hungry peoples from settling in Egypt, and parties of Meshwesh filtered across the borders taking service as mercenaries in the Egyptian armies and forming an influential military caste. Their descendants became powerful enough to intervene decisively in Egyptian affairs and form two dynasties of their own.

The removal of the immediate threat from Libya, allowed Ramesses III to marshal all his reserves to meet a mass incursion by land and sea on the eastern border. This great migration of Sea-peoples had already surged through Syria spreading destruction afar, while the Hittites in Anatolia had been overwhelmed by Phrygian invaders. The Egyptian land forces met this new horde in Phoenicia and managed to beat it back, though not for long, since, soon after the reign of Ramesses III, we find the Philistines and Teucrians in possession of the coastal areas of Palestine. The invading fleet was caught off one of the Nile mouths and in the first great sea-battle of which we have details, largely destroyed. These defensive wars

c. 1300 B.C.

c. 1219 B.C.

c. 1174 and
1167 B.C.

Plate 60

940–730 B.C.

c. 1170 B.C.

succeeded in keeping the borders of Egypt inviolate but the buffer-possessions in Asia had to be abandoned by the successors of Ramesses III. Egypt, in fact, secured her integrity at some cost. She escaped the transfusions of new blood and ideas, such as rejuvenated the peoples of Canaan and created the vigorous Phoenician city-states. Thereafter she lived on, a Bronze Age anachronism in a world that steadily moved away from her.

The civilization of the New Kingdom seems the most golden of all the epochs of Egyptian history, and the nearest to us, probably because of the wealth of its remains. Its great Pharaohs are more than mere names; we have many of their personal possessions, their sceptres, weapons, chariots, jewels, and finery, their very paint-boxes and toys. We can even look upon the now shrunken features that once held the world in awe. Its voices are many and varied: we have the measured strophes of the great paeans of Tuthmosis III and Merenptah, the psalm-like sentiments of Akhenaten's hymns to the Aten, and the nearest approach to an epic that the Egyptian poet ever achieved in the account of the valour of Ramesses II at the Battle of Kadesh. There are joyous poems in praise of the coronations of kings and the wonderful cities they had built: and lyric verses to be sung to the lute describing the pangs of separated lovers, or their delight in each other's company in some Oriental pleasance. A tomb-painting in the British Museum showing singers and dancers at a banquet, has the charming words of their eternal spring-song above them:

Fig. 1

The Earth-god has implanted his beauty in every body.
The Creator has done this with his two hands as
                                    balm to his heart.
The channels are filled with water anew
And the land is flooded with his love.

A more satirical note is struck in allegories such as *The Blinding of Truth by Falsehood* or *The Dispute between Body and Head* or in the miscellanies praising the profession of the scribe at the expense of other callings, or in *A Literary Controversy* which exposes the pretensions of one pundit and the learning of his rival. In a slightly less irreverent vein are the vulgarizations in the form of folk-tales of religious myths such as *The Tale of Two Brothers, The Outwitting of Re by Isis,* and the Rabelaisian *Contendings of Horus and Seth.* The wars of liberation and conquest engendered a crop of popular historical romances such as *Apophis and Seken-en-re* and *The Taking of Joppa,* besides the fairy-tales set in Syria such as *The Foredoomed Prince.* In addition to these literary works, there are autobiographies, model letters, books of proverbs and maxims in the tradition of the 'teachings' of earlier ages, accounts, taxation-rolls, horoscopes, dream interpretations, a sadly damaged list of kings, and a body of juridical papyri dealing with law-suits, wills, marriage settlements, a curious case of adoption, and the report of a Royal Commission which investigated the harem conspiracy that appears to have ended the life of Ramesses III, and the proceedings of other tribunals which looked into allega-tions of widespread tomb-robbery during the reigns of the last Ramessides. Probably in this same category is to be put *The Adventures of Wen-amun,* an account of misfortunes that befell a priest of Amun when he set forth for Lebanon in the sunset years of the New Kingdom to buy cedar-wood for the barque

Plate 53

of Amun. For its vivid character-drawing and descriptive force, this narrative is unequalled in all the literature of the pre-Classical world.

Plates 57, 50

The artistic legacy is vast, from colossal statues in granite and quartzite to small articles of luxury in ivory and gold. New materials make their appearance. A factory for the manufacture of vessels in brilliant polychrome glass seems to have been attached to the Royal palaces; and great skill was shown in

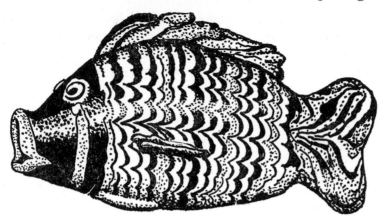

Fig. 42   Bottle in the form of a Nile fish of white, yellow, black and blue opaque glass
from Amarna, now in the British Museum; c. 1350 B.C. Length 3¾ in.

casting glass to imitate semi-precious stones for inlay in jewellery and furniture. Fine work in various coloured faiences is a prominent feature of architectural decoration especially during Ramesside times. The art of the goldsmith hardly reaches the high standard of the Court jewellers of Dynasty XII, but a process of colouring gold in tones from pink to crimson was invented during this period. Tapestry-weaving and needlework embroidery were employed for the new and luxurious fashions of dress, though the surviving examples are in poor condition. The rich store of treasure from the tomb of Tut-ankh-amun has given us a dazzling conspectus of Court art at the period of its most opulent development, and acquainted us with the skill and resource of the craftsmen of the day whose taste was often a little too exuberantly rococo.

Plates 64–6

Plate 48

All this heritage has survived by the accident that the founders of the New Kingdom were princes of Thebes who made that city their main capital, lavished much of their wealth upon its god Amun, and were buried there after death. The tradition begun by Amenophis I of abandoning the

Plate 61

pyramid in favour of a rock-hewn sepulchre in the crags of
Western Thebes was followed by his successors who for the
next four centuries cut their tombs in the lonely Valley of the
Tombs of the Kings and built their mortuary temples on the
plain below. Other *wadis* were subsequently used for the tombs
of some queens and princes. In the adjacent hills the Court
officials were granted burial in the old tradition and the painted
walls of their chapels have bequeathed us a most lively picture
of life in Dynasty XVIII—the reception by the Pharaoh at
his accession and jubilees of ambassadors bringing gifts from
Libya, Syria, Palestine, and the Aegean; the royal investitures;
scenes of military life and the professional occupations of the
owners; besides such traditional subjects as the hunt in marsh
and *wadi*; the procession to the tomb and the last rites. After
the Amarna interlude, the subjects lose their pagan delight in
the world and its joys and show a more sombre preoccupation
with funerary scenes and magic rites, in this probably being
influenced by the decoration of contemporary Royal tombs as
well as by a change of mood. To cater for this large clientele a
village grew up at what is now Deir el-Medina housing
generations of necropolis workers; and it is from the ruins of
this hamlet that the vast majority of the Theban objects in our
museums have come. We owe the preservation of the New
Kingdom past almost entirely to the dry climate of Thebes.

The Pharaohs of Dynasty XVIII followed tradition in
having a Northern Residence as well near Memphis, and the
embellishment of Thebes really began with Queen Hatshepsut
who, as the heiress queen, usurped supreme power in default of
male claimants of pure descent and made the 'Two Lands to
labour with bowed back for her'. She was particularly devoted
to the worship of Amun, whose oracle doubtless sanctioned
her seizure of power, and built a splendid temple dedicated to
him and her own funerary cult at Deir el-Bahri. Her architect
and favourite, Sennemut, was obviously influenced by the

Plate 56

Plate 51
Figs. 46, 47

Fig. 14

Plate 39

Plate 38
Plate 40

Fig. 43 Detail of a panel in a tunic of Tut-ankh-amun, now in Cairo, showing a hunt of gazelle and ibex with dogs, embroidered in coloured threads on an open-weave linen ground; c. 1345 B.C. Height 6 in.

Fig. 37

adjacent temple of Menthu-hotep I but transformed the design of his predecessor into a much bolder and more satisfactory architectural entity which though greatly ruined still survives as one of the most impressive buildings of Ancient Egypt. The architects and sculptors trained on Hatshepsut's pioneer constructions were available for the undertakings of her

Plate 41

successor, Tuthmosis III, in whose long reign the buoyancy of the new Egypt, confident and wealthy as a result of its military successes, is expressed in widespread building. The climax

Plate 42

of this development was reached in the reign of Amenophis III who devoted most of his reign of nearly forty years to the arts of peace. His buildings at Thebes are still impressive, even in their ruins, though they were once lavishly decorated with gold and silver; and in addition we read of 'numerous royal statues in granite of Elephantine, in quartzite and every splendid and costly stone, established as everlasting memorials and shining in the faces of men like the morning sun'. He furnished the temple of Mut, the consort of Amun, with some six hundred statues of the lion-headed goddess Sekhmet and examples of these sculptures, usually usurped by later kings, are in nearly every Egyptological collection. With him statuary on an enormous scale makes its appearance, the most notable perhaps being the pair of colossi still dominating the Theban plain before the vanished portal of his funerary temple demolished by Merenptah. The Northern specimen, known as the Colossus of Memnon, was famous in Classical times for its song at sunrise until an earth tremor nudged it into silence in

c. A.D. 200

the reign of Septimius Severus. The temple of Amenophis III at Luxor is still standing, and the fame of this and other

Plate 49

great monuments won for the King's Master of Works, Amenophis-son-of-Hapu, the unprecedented honour of a funerary temple in his lifetime and deification in the Ptolemaic Period.

All this splendour fell into decay during the short but

disastrous reign of Akhenaten culminating in his insane persecution of Amun when the god's name and figure were hammered out of every monument however insignificant. Afterwards when Tut⸁ankh⸁amun attempted to return to the policies of the past, he reports that the temples of the land from South to North were abandoned, weeds grew in their sanctu⸁ aries and their courtyards were as a trodden path. It was left, however, to the Ramessides of the next dynasty to repair much of the damage, Sethos I restoring desecrated buildings at Thebes and embellishing Abydos and other centres. His son, Ramesses II, was the most vigorous builder to have worn the double crown, nearly half the temples remaining in Egypt dating from his reign. His mortuary temple at Thebes, popu⸁ larly known as the Ramesseum, the huge Hypostyle Hall at Karnak, the rock⸁hewn temple at Abu Simbel, and many other erections, would have contented lesser men: but in addition he indulged in a kind of landscape gardening, hauling the usurped statues and monuments of earlier kings to adorn the new capital city of Pi⸁Ramesse on which he expended so much treasure. Much of his work, particularly of the latter half of his long reign, is coarse, tasteless, and tired, but he left so universal and impressive a legend of superhuman qualities that his successors could only attempt a pale reflexion of it. Ramesses III, for instance, named his sons after those of his idol, and in his mortuary temple at Medinet Habu copied much of the decoration and texts of the Ramesseum, though the reliefs showing the King hunting wild beasts and human foes seem to be original in design. This temple included in its complex a palace, administrative buildings, military quarters, store⸁rooms, gardens, and pools. It was enclosed by a great wall and the main entrance was a fortified gate⸁building like a Syrian *migdol*. It served, in fact, as a fortress for the protection of the population of West Thebes in times of trouble during the later years of Dynasty XX. It was eventually taken 'by

Plate 46

Plate 48

Plate 54

Plates 56, 57

Plate 30

Plate 58

Plates 59, 60

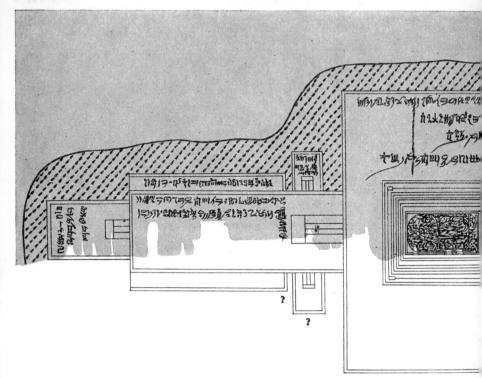

Fig. 44   Part of an ancient plan drawn on papyrus of the tomb of Ramesses IV in the Valley of the Kings a
by fives brines and a pall) and store-rooms. The hieratic captions give descriptions and measurements of th

foreigners' at the end of the dynasty, but whether these were
the Nubian troops of the Viceroy of Kush who stepped in to
c. 1085 B.C. put down a rebellion in Middle Egypt and perhaps also of the
High Priest of Amun, or simply marauding Libyans, we
cannot yet tell.

This lawlessness is but one sign among many of the decline
in public affairs that gathered momentum during Dynasty XX;
yet the Royal sepulchres continue to be vast excavations. The
architect's plan of the tomb of Ramesses IV, which has survived on a papyrus in Turin, shows that it was meant to be

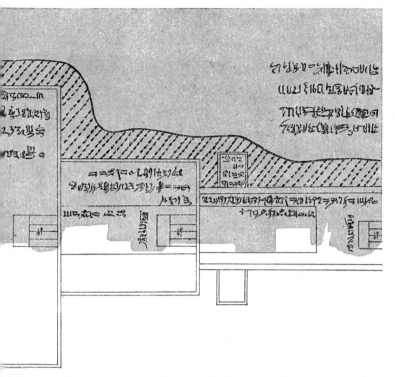

the main corridor, ante-chamber, burial chamber (with a plan of the sarcophagus surrounded ; after a papyrus in the Turin Museum; c. 1140 B.C. Scale, 2 : 7

equipped with a full set of furniture, including five gold-covered tabernacles around the great granite sarcophagus, similar to the opulent provision made for Tut-ankh-amun. The fine granite sarcophagus made for this same King, and the one for his father Ramesses III, testify to the vigour of the Pharaonic tradition which could still command such resources in what seems to be a period of decline.

Under their fighting Pharaohs the Egyptians in Early Dynasty XVIII had shown a new-found zest for war. The professional soldier, as distinct from the unwilling, conscripted

Plate 58

peasant, had made a sudden appearance. The Asiatic campaigns introduced many exotic novelties to the Nile Valley, strange peoples, fashions of dress, Canaanite words and expressions, foreign cults such as those of Baal, Resheph, and Astarte. It was from Syria that Tuthmosis III introduced curious plants and animals to adorn the botanical gardens he built at Thebes. In all this, the Egyptian horizons were widened and an optimistic spirit prevailed. But by the reign of Amenophis III the inevitable victories of the war-machine had bred a complacent acceptance of success which ill fitted the Egyptian to cope with the set-backs of the latter half of the period. The Egyptian tended to leave the military career to ambitious foreigners and his Army soon came to be manned largely by mercenaries—Nubians, Sudanis, Canaanites, Sardinians, Libyans, and others. Asiatics rose to high office in the State, one of them being virtual ruler of Egypt at the end of Dynasty XIX. The Egyptians turned more to the professions of priest and scribe, being content to fill or create some comfortable bureaucratic office which they could hand on to their sons.

1380 B.C.

Fig. 52

This lack of enterprise is but one symptom of a gradual ossification in Egyptian society and a conforming view of life that increasingly sicklies over the whole cast of Egyptian thought. The old feudal society with its amateur officials had been replaced by the professional soldiers, priests, and officials, with a consequent submission of the individual to a bureaucratic system. The change is more evident in tomb-chapels of the age, where gay scenes of everyday life are discarded in Ramesside times in favour of the accepted icons of a dark, funerary mythology. The self-contained burial of Hyksos times had been elaborated in the wealthy days of Dynasty XVIII, nests of coffins, stone sarcophagi, Canopic chests, funerary papyri, and the personal possessions of the deceased being housed in the burial chamber. But as the period wore on there was a return to the former practice, until in all but the wealthiest burials, only a coffin, or set of coffins, was provided, painted with selected religious scenes and texts; and this, with variations in style, became the tradition for burial in subsequent periods of Pharaonic Egypt. A copy of *The Book of the Dead* and an armoury of amulets and shawabti-figures might also be provided, because the accent now was on the apparatus of magic. Technique to some extent had replaced conviction.

CHAPTER VIII

Decline and Eclipse during the Late Period

Dynasties XXI–XXXI, 1075–332 B.C.

Plate 67

THE NEWS FROM THEBES in the last years of Dynasty XX tells a story of universal decay. The Pharaohs in Pi-Ramesse seem seldom to have visited their Southern capital and the governorship of the Thebaid passed to the heavenly king Amun-re who promulgated his oracular edicts through his priesthood with the First Prophet, or High Priest, at their head. In Western Asia the coast of Palestine was firmly in the hands of Philistines whose monopoly of iron secured them a superiority in weapons. The mastery of the seas was passing to the Canaanites of Phoenicia. The unemployment among a professional soldiery composed largely of mercenaries increased the tale of lawlessness. In such a situation, exacerbated by famines caused by low Niles, it is not surprising that the records reveal gross dishonesty among officials concerned only with concealing their own shortcomings, and strikes and violence among the lower orders driven desperate by hunger. But the most important factor was the eclipse of the Pharaoh as the god who ruled men (see below, p. 165). The tombs of the kings at Thebes with their fabulous hoards of treasure had always tempted desperate men to rob them. Now they appear to have been systematically pillaged probably with the connivance of the officials in charge so that out of some thirty kings' tombs only the deposit of Tut-ankh-amun remained largely intact, probably because as a heretic, his name had been expunged from the necropolis records.

The Egyptians, so ebullient and sanguine in the Early

Date B.C. and Years of Reign		Principal Kings	Chief Centres	Foreign Affairs	Significant Events
1075		DYNASTY XXI		Dorian invasions of	Leadership of
	45	Psusennes I	Tanis	Greece. Growth	Delta
			Thebes	of Phoenicia	
				Rise of Israel	Libyan mercenaries
940		DYNASTIES XXII–XXIII			achieve supremacy
	21	Sesonchis I	Bubastis	Sack of Temple at	Kush independent
	36	Osorkon	Tanis	Jerusalem	Skill in metal- and
	54	Pedubast	Thebes		faience-work
			Herakleopolis		Rising anarchy in
830		DYNASTY XXIV		Revival of Assyrian	Egypt provokes
	5	Bocchoris	Sais	power under	intervention of
				Tiglath-Pileser III	Kush
751		DYNASTY XXV			Amun-cult domin-
	35	Pi-ankhy	Napata (Sudan)		ant at Napata and
	15	Shabako	Thebes	Invasions of	Thebes. Rebuild-
	20	Shebitku	Tanis	Egypt by Assyrians	ing at Thebes
	26	Taharqa		Sack of Thebes	and elsewhere
				Expulsion of	Antiquarian study
664		DYNASTY XXVI		Kushites	of the past
	54	Psammetichos I	Sais	Independence from	Revival in arts
	15	Necho II	Edfu	Assyrians achieved	and crafts
	6	Psammetichos II	Saqqara	Excursions into	Eclipse of Amun
	19	Apries (Hophra)	Daphnae	Phoenicia. Trade	Philhellenism
	44	Amasis	Naukratis	with Greece. Anti-	Greek mercenaries
				Persian intrigues	in pay of kings
525–404		DYNASTY XXVII (Persians)		Conquest of Egypt	
				by Cambyses	
404–398		DYNASTY XXVIII			Resistance to
	7	Amyrteos	Sais	Eventual liberation	Persians weakened
				with Greek aid	by dynastic
398–378		DYNASTY XXIX		Alliances against	squabbles
	13	Achoris	Mendes	Persia	Last flourish of
					native arts
378–341		DYNASTY XXX	Sebennytos	Repulse of Persian	
	19	Nectanebo I	Bubastis	invasion (Phanar-	The last native
	19	Nectanebo II	Edfu	barzus) 373 B.C.	Pharaoh
341–333		DYNASTY XXXI (Persians)		Reconquest of	
				Egypt by Persians	
332		Alexander of Macedon conquers Persian Empire			

Table H Late Period (Dynasties XXI to XXXI)

Dynasty XVIII, had lost heart. Respect for the kingship still survived more as a superstition than an article of faith, but the monarchy was transformed thereafter into a military dictatorship depending for its stability upon mercenaries; and successive dynasties of Libyans, Kushites, Persians, Greeks, and Romans held power for as long as they could sustain it by force of arms against rival claimants.

Plate 69

With the obscure death of Ramesses XI the country fell into its natural halves, with one dynasty ruling at Tanis, and a military family who had got themselves appointed to the highest offices in the hierarchy of Amun ruling at Thebes. The intermarriage of these two families reunited Upper and Lower Egypt under one king but the union was only nominal, and thereafter a separate rule was exercised in the Thebaid by Amun-re and his human agents. The tendency was for both Upper and Lower Egypt to split into independent city-states whenever the central power declined, as it did with a regular rhythm. Each new dynasty began with vigour and promise, reviving the old dream of an Asiatic empire, as the Old Testament reveals, and interfering in the turbulent politics of the area as opportunity served. Their campaigns, however, were little better than armed raids, winning a temporary glory. Whenever the Egyptian forces came up against a battle-trained and united enemy with superior weapons such as the Assyrians, Babylonians, and Persians, they invariably suffered. Constant defeat could not but produce further discouragement at home as well as the reputation abroad of being a broken reed.

In 940 B.C. a family of Libyan descent, who had settled at Herakleopolis, became influential enough to be favoured by the Tanite kings and succeeded them as Dynasty XXII. The first of the line, the energetic Sesonchis (Shishak) invaded Palestine and plundered Solomon's temple of its rich treasure, restoring a little of Egypt's prestige. But the Libyan dynasties

Plate 72

ended in dissension and fission, so that when the Kushite king,

Pi-ankhy, marched from Napata to capture Egypt in the name of order and orthodoxy, he met with no united resistance. Since the end of Dynasty XX, Nubia and Kush, the Biblical Ethiopia, had gradually become an independent State with its capital at Napata where the cult of Amun-re was strictly observed. The pious Kushite kings favoured a provincial version of the Egyptian culture of a purer past, harking back to the classical arts of the Middle Kingdom. They proved energetic builders, particularly at Thebes, and brought some direction into the affairs of Egypt though the country was far from being united under their sway, as the prophet Isaiah[1] knew well enough. The intrigues of Taharqa, the son of Pi-ankhy, at length brought about a long-delayed show-down with the Assyrians whose forces twice marched into Egypt, eventually sacking Thebes and driving Taharqa's successor, Tanwetamani, into his own Kushite domains, where he and his successors became more and more Africanized and ceased to play any direct role in Egyptian affairs.

Plate 73
c. 670 B.C.

The Kushites continued a policy, begun by a Libyan pre-decessor, Osorkon III, of neutralizing the powerful *imperium in imperio* of Thebes by appointing one of the royal women as the Divine Consort of Amun. Pi-ankhy obliged the Divine Consort Shepen-wepet I to adopt his sister Amenirdas I; and this practice of making the chief office in the Sacred College elective rather than hereditary was continued by succeeding dynasties. Such consorts ruled with the assistance of their stewards, the most notable being Menthu-em-het who not only governed Thebes in the difficult days of the Assyrian invasions, but was one of the chief patrons of the new art that flourished in the interludes between the Persian conquests.

Plate 75

Plate 74

The longest of these Indian summers belongs to Dynasty XXVI, when a Lower Egyptian family originating in Sais brought more than a century of order and prosperity to the

664-525 B.C.

[1] *Isaiah*, XIX, 2.

troubled land. The first Psammetichos freed himself from the overlordship of Assyria which was now beset with its own troubles. In their stirring days the Saites were to see the sack of their own 'populous No [Thebes] that was situate among the rivers'[1] repeated in the destruction of Nineveh and Babylon. Psammetichos I had his daughter adopted as the successor of the Divine Consort, and appointed his own men to key positions in Edfu and Herakleopolis to keep Thebes in check. He also curbed the power of the Libyan military caste by employing Ionian, Carian, and Lydian mercenaries. With this *corps d'élite* and the possession of a strong fleet, probably largely Phoenician, the Saites ruled as merchant princes, restoring prosperity by active commercial ventures, forming factories for Milesians at Daphnae and Naukratis, and setting a precedent for the export of Egyptian corn and wool which was to be followed with greater intensity by the Ptolemies. In the interests of trade, Necho began a canal from the Nile to the Red Sea and commissioned Phoenicians to circumnavigate Africa. But the Saites never won the whole-hearted co-operation of their subjects by these policies. The favouritism shown to Greek oracles, wives, traders, and soldiers aroused jealousy and revolt, and when the Persian Cambyses invaded the country it fell into his hands without much trouble. The Persians, who organized their Empire with a thoroughness lacking in previous conquerors, ruled Egypt with the aid of efficient collaborators for nearly two centuries, except for an interlude when native princes with Greek aid were able to snatch half a century of independence. This was, however, the last twitch of dying Pharaonic Egypt, and it was only the embalmed corpse that then passed in turn to the Persian kings, the Greek Ptolemies, and the Roman emperors.

Since the Residence Cities of Late Period kings have suffered almost total destruction or lie beneath Delta silt, the

Plates 76, 77

525 B.C.

Plate 80

[1] *Nahum*, III, 8.

absence of material remains from the palace sites is apt to sharpen our impression of decline and poverty. Yet there are indications that whenever a new dynasty attained to vigour and wealth, Court patronage could still stimulate the cunning fingers of Egyptian craftsmen to produce works of art which are often of considerable merit. The Royal burials at Tanis have shown that besides heirlooms and usurpations of an earlier age, the contemporary art could still maintain a good standard of design and technique. During the Libyan dynasties a school of Palace artists flourished who showed considerable skill in the working of bronze, silver, and gold, though little of the latter work has survived. Perhaps it was the same craftsmen who produced blue faience footed cups or 'chalices' strongly influenced by the shape and design of engraved metal prototypes, which are of such excellence that they have often been accredited to Dynasty XVIII, though a specimen in Berlin and a fragment at Eton bearing names of Libyan kings show to which era they belong.

Plate 69

Plates 70, 71

Plate 68

   The Kushite kings with their conservative tastes for classical standards are usually adjudged to be the instigators of the antiquarian study of the past which is such a feature of the following dynasties, but the faience panels from a shrine of Dynasty XXIII, show that the movement began earlier. Looking back in nostalgia is in fact the *malaise* of the entire Late Period which recalled former grandeurs as the ideals to which it could only aspire. The intensive copying of the past is a feature of the Saite Age—though the tomb-reliefs of Menthu-em-het and his temple statues had already set the pace—and sculpture in the style and dress of all periods, but particularly that of the Old and Middle Kingdoms, was produced with enough fidelity to deceive some modern observers, though to the trained eye the deception is fairly obvious, the Saite versions having a high surface-working and a lack of inner conviction. Nevertheless, as an idealistic,

Plate 72

Plates 78-81

academic art it has its appeal. Its technique, especially in the cutting of inscriptions in hard stones, is faultless, but as in all art where style has become more important than content, a tendency to emphasize the abstractions underlying form leads to a distinctive mannerism. Egypt had invariably gone back to her past as a point of vigorous departure, but now her return was a permanent retreat from the world of her decline. That monasticism which is so characteristic of Christian Egypt is already inherent in the outlook of the Late Period. In Persian and especially in Ptolemaic times, the dying embers of this art were to glow for a brief interval when a somewhat incongruous realistic portraiture was grafted on the idealistic and abstract forms of Saite art, but that manifestation lies outside the scope of this limited survey.

CHAPTER IX

Ancient Egyptian Society

I. THE KING

THE OFT-QUOTED EPIGRAM of Hecataeus, that Egypt is the gift of the Nile, is still true, but Ancient Egypt was no less the creation of the Pharaoh. The origins of the kingship go back to prehistoric days when the nomads of North Africa were still dependent upon rain for the fertility of their pastures, their herds, and themselves, and rain-makers played a vital role in tribal life. The earliest kings are shown in the habit of a pastoral chieftain, carrying the crook and flail-like *ladanisterion*, wearing an animal tail at their backs, and the beard of their goat-flocks on their chins. For solemn occasions this remained their ceremonial dress throughout history. Like all such divine kings, in prehistoric times they were ritually killed when their powers began to wane, and their corpses were probably dismembered and buried, or burnt and the ashes scattered for the greater fertility of the land. By historic times this savage rite had been replaced by such magic ceremonies designed to rejuvenate the monarch as the Jubilee Festival, or substitutes were provided such as animals, mock-kings, and probably persons drowned by chance in the Nile. But the tradition that the king should die for his people persisted in folk-lore and in the more primitive spells of *The Pyramid Texts*; and there are anthropologists who believe that the ceremonial killing of the Pharaoh was sometimes revived in moments of crisis, as with the last ruler of Egypt, Cleopatra, who ended her life by means of the personal god of the king, the uraeus.

The functions of kingship are seen quite clearly at the very start of Pharaonic Egypt on a mace-head and a ceremonial palette, both originally from Hierakonpolis. On the former,

Plates 5, 7, 54

Plates 7, 20, 23

Fig. 45 Scene in relief on a fragmentary votive limestone mace-head, excavated at Hierakonpolis and now at Oxford, showing King Scorpion performing an agricultural rite. In the background are standards from which hang lapwings symbolizing the people of Egypt, and a bow representing a foreign people; c. 3120 B.C. Scale, 3 : 8

King Scorpion is shown performing a solemn rite, subsequently associated with the Osirian shawabti-figures, of clearing the irrigation channels after the receding of the inundation and spreading the fertile silt over the fields. The prehistoric rain-maker who kept his tribe, their crops, and beasts in good health by exercising a magic control over the weather, has thus been transformed into the Pharaoh, able to sustain the entire nation by having command over the Nile flood. From now on, the kingship and the Nile are intimately associated. Even Akhenaten, whose sole god was a sun-god, is apostrophized as 'this myriad of Niles', and as 'a Nile which flows daily giving life to Egypt'. Several instances exist where the Pharaohs acted as water-diviners when wells had to be dug in desert places. Ramesses II was thought to have special influence over the elements even in the far-off lands of the Hittites, where he could make rain fall or withhold it at his pleasure. This power over water (and what was rain but a Nile set in the sky by a beneficent god for those lesser nations that did not enjoy a terrestrial Nile!) was supposed not to cease with a king's death but to be transferred to Osiris with whom the deceased had mingled.

It is scarcely an exaggeration to claim for the other antiquity from Hierakonpolis, the palette of King Narmer, that it is the most important Pharaonic monument to have been discovered in Egypt. Here in essence is expressed the entire character of the kingship, its symbols, its dogma, and its art. The King's name appears at the top within a palace building and is flanked by the heads of Hathor with her woman's face emerging from a cow's head, so representing a complicated concept of the sky as a star-speckled cow and the foster-mother of mankind and also the mother of the sky-god Horus of whom the King is an incarnation. The reverse, illustrated in Plate 5, shows Narmer as a figure of heroic proportions in his medicine-man's garb, frozen into a stance which was to remain sacrosanct for as long as Pharaonic art persisted, and sacrificing a foe before a rebus of the hawk-god Horus leading captive a marsh-land. Below, two Asiatics[1] lie fallen. The other side of the palette shows further scenes of victory, and the whole object commemorates the divine might of Narmer who triumphs over foreign enemies as well as rebels at home. The same theme is expressed a little more symbolically on the Scorpion mace-head where in the background standards appear with lapwings and bows hanging from them. On a statue-base from the Step Pyramid, Djoser is shown treading down nine bows symbolizing the neighbours of Egypt, and being worshipped by submissive lapwings representing the native populace. At this

Plate 5

cf. Plate 68

cf. Plate 66

[1] Y. Yadin: *Israel Exploration Journal*, v, pp. 1–16.

early stage, there is no distinction between the peoples of Egypt and those of adjacent lands who are all prostrate beneath the Pharaoh as an omnipotent god. The disproportionate sizes of the King, his subjects, and even the image of the god, upon these early monuments clearly show that the Pharaoh is to be regarded as a universal god in his own right rather than the human agent of a god. It is in this that Egypt presents us with a typically African solution of political problems. The other high civilizations that had arisen in river valleys during the Bronze Age and knew the arts of writing and recording, remained a congeries of rival city-states while Egypt displayed a national conformity personified in her divine king. For the Pharaoh is the classic example of the god incarnate as king. In Egypt in the earliest period he is perhaps to be regarded as 'the Greatest God' after whose human image the other gods gradually transpose themselves from their primitive animal or fetishistic forms in the manner of Hathor. The idea of a tangible god appealed particularly to the Egyptian need for a concrete image of reality, but the divine influence of the Pharaoh was recognized far afield in a world which had little of nationalism in its loyalties. The Pharaoh claimed sovereignty over Egyptian and foreigner alike, and both combined to do him homage at his advent. The painted walls of the Theban tomb-chapels of the New Kingdom have left us the clearest pictures of this ceremony when princes from Asia and Africa and the 'Isles of the Great Green' set out on a Magi-like journey to lay their gifts at the feet of the newly crowned king, and beg

Plate 51

from him 'the breath of life', uniting in this devotion with the people of Egypt itself. The bows and lapwings on the monuments of Scorpion, and the designs on the palette of Narmer, suggest that this relationship between Pharaoh and mortals had existed from the dawn of history at least.

Large-scale irrigation and land-reclamation projects do not seem to have been inaugurated until a centralized State under the rule of a sole king had been developed. The earliest kings were associated with the control of the flood-waters, and the dramatic change that the political unification of Egypt must have effected in co-ordinating and accelerating all kinds of activities may at the time have seemed miraculous. Just as the destructive power of the inundation could be transformed into a beneficent force, so by the same Pharaonic control the affairs of men could be regulated for good. The precedents created by Narmer were followed by his successors not as a recipe for success but as part of an inevitable order. The king was the personification of *ma'at*, a word which we translate as 'rightness' or 'truth' or 'justice', but which also seems to have the meaning of 'the natural cosmic order'. The forces of evil could upset *ma'at* until restoration had been effected by some appropriate act—a magic rite, or the advent of a new king. The means by which the king established *ma'at* were his 'Authoritative Utterance' and his 'Understanding'. Since he ruled as a god, all things, all persons were his, and the law was his pro-nouncement. This does not mean that he ruled arbitrarily, though it was a fiction that he consulted only his own 'heart'; also he might take heed of the oracle of a god. A necessarily heavy weight of precedent formed the body of *ma'at*, so that it was only occasionally that the Pharaoh could boast of some-thing the like of which had not been done since the primeval time when the gods ruled. The strict regulation of the Pharaoh's life is suggested by the words of Diodorus: 'For there was a set time not only for his holding audience or rendering judgement, but even for his taking a walk, bathing and sleeping with his wife; in short, for every act of his life.'

This concept of the Pharaoh as the god Horus incarnate reached its fullest development in the Early Old Kingdom, and probably the Step Pyramid and the pyramids at Giza stand as its greatest memorials when the entire nation under-took the tremendous activity involved in raising and equipping these giant monuments not for the sole benefit of their human ruler, but to ensure the persistence of their greatest divinity with which their very existence was identified. But already during Dynasty IV the influence of Heliopolis was making itself felt and became dominant in the next dynasty. The Pharaoh now came to be regarded as a descendant of the sun-god Re who had ruled Egypt in the beginning. There was a subtle shift of emphasis from the idea of an incarnation to the idea of the physical son of a god. A folk-story, for instance, concerned with the founding of Dynasty V explains how Re fathered the first kings of this dynasty upon the wife of a mere High Priest of Heliopolis. By the end of the Old Kingdom, however, another aspect was also being emphasized and the living Pharaoh was regarded as an incarnation of the great god Horus who on death became Osiris while his son stood in his place as the new Horus. The kingship, rather than its incumbent, was immortal, the Egyptian universe being created anew in the old pattern with each change of king. This cosmogony was reinforced by the Osirian myth which taught that an ancient divine king had suffered death and dismemberment but arose from the dead to be king and judge in the underworld, while his posthumously begotten son Horus ruled in his father's stead on earth.

cf. Plate 72

The concept of the king as the supreme god incarnate was sadly weakened during the First Intermediate Period when the exclusiveness of the Pharaoh was replaced by a multiplicity of local kinglets who boasted less of their divinity than of their ability to preserve their people by their temporal might. This concern for the material well-being of their subjects was carried over into the tenets of government during the Middle Kingdom when the idea took hold that the king tended his subjects as a good shepherd watched his flock. 'For God has made me the herdsman of this land for he knew that I would maintain it in order for him', said Sesostris I to his assembled courtiers. 'He is possessed of graciousness, rich in benignity, and through love has he conquered', said Sinuhe of this same King. Though the Pharaohs of Dynasty XII restored the prestige of the kingship it was more as an invincible champion than as a god that the 'Living Horus' was regarded. Much of the reverence for the Pharaoh as the greater-god-to-be had passed to that deification of kingship, Osiris, despite the weight of a tradition that still gave the terrestrial ruler and his family sumptuous burial in a pyramid-tomb.

The kings of Dynasties XVII and XVIII had to fight their way to power by hard campaigning against all rivals, and with their eventual triumph they found themselves ruling with unchallenged authority. The character of the monarchy during the New Kingdom is distinctly martial. The Pharaoh himself took the field at the head of his troops and it is as a divine war-lord, the incarnation of Menthu or Baal, that he now appears. His heroic stature is carefully emphasized by his prowess in rowing, shooting, riding, and hunting. It is a convention that he should disregard the cautious advice of his counsellors and devise a bold and dangerous plan which is crowned with resounding success. The victories of the military genius Tuthmosis III raised the authority of the kingship to new heights and it is his vizier Rekhmire who refers to the king as 'the god by whose guidance men live, the father and mother of mankind, unique, without a peer'. Similarly, the father-in-law of Akhenaten refers to him as 'this god who made me'. With Amenophis III and his colossal monuments, such as the temple at Soleb where he worships himself among other gods, the kingship reached the high-water mark of its prestige during the New Kingdom. His son Amenophis IV who, in deference to his promotion of the cult of the sun-god, the Aten, changed his name to Akhenaten, created his god in the king's image. The Aten was the heavenly king *par excellence*, and the Pharaoh was at once his son and co-regent

Fig. 4, Plate 48

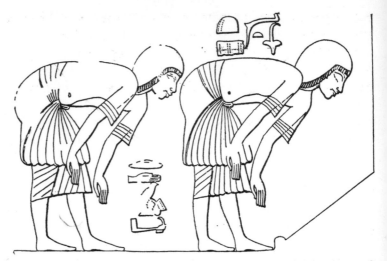

Fig. 46   Officials of the royal harem bending low in the presence of the royal pair; after a relief in the tomb of Ramose No. 55 at Thebes; c. 1368 B.C. Scale, 1 : 9

in whose presence the courtiers bow lower than ever before. Parallels with the old sun-cult of Heliopolis can be traced in this concept; what was new was the insistence that the Aten was intangible and the only god. Monotheism was a novel and alien idea in Egypt which instinctively tolerated so many diverse and concrete forms of deity; yet the authority of the Pharaoh was such that even this revolutionary principle was apparently accepted, if not understood, by a devout people who dutifully hammered out the name of the rival heavenly king Amun and his consort and suppressed the plural form of 'god' wherever they appeared.

Plate 46

This vicious persecution of Amun and other cults may in fact give us the clue to the true character of this curious interlude in Egyptian history. The god incarnate was unfortunately subject to the ills that mortal flesh is heir to. Amenophis III suffered miserably from dental caries; Siptah had a club foot; Ramesses V died of smallpox; Merenptah was grossly obese.

Akhenaten presents us with the unique case of a Pharaoh who did not abide by the rules, and could only have flouted them because he was not fully sane, though until the skull believed to be his is re-subjected to expert examination by pathologists the absolute proof will be lacking. At least he was given a quiet and quasi-private burial at Thebes by his intimates. A few years afterwards, his successor Tut-ankh-amun described the conditions that faced him when he came to the throne with *ma'at* (see p. 161, above) overthrown, the temples neglected, the priesthoods dispersed, the people de-moralized, lacking divine comfort and direction, and the armies of Egypt defeated abroad. The picture is traditionally overdrawn but the failure of Akhenaten must have dealt a considerable blow to the idea of the infallible character of the kingship in Egypt, for a decade later we find that the widow of Tut-ankh-amun is demeaning herself, as she confesses, by asking for a Hittite prince to become her consort, and therefore Pharaoh, so as to carry on the line of Ahmosis, the chastiser of Asiatics.

Plate 48

The kingship during the New Kingdom was closely identified with the military policies of conquest abroad and keeping inviolate the borders of Egypt. It was a concept geared only to success and could but decline as the affairs of Egypt herself began to totter. New and vigorous races with superior weapons challenged successfully her military supremacy; dynastic squabbles, low Niles, and increasing impoverishment dealt the idea a mortal blow. In the Late Period the kingship became but a prize for which foreigners—Libyans, 'Ethiopians', Persians, and Greeks—fought each other. While the weight of traditional thought made it certain that there would always be tremendous respect paid to the kingship especially in Court circles, the fact is that men turned more to the worship of gods in the form of kings, to Amun, Re-Harakhte, and Osiris. Prayers were addressed to gods less and less through the intermediary of the king and more through the agency of the city-god, while for the great mass of the people, as the cult of the god incarnate in the king declined, the worship of animals increased to grotesque proportions.[1] The greatness of Ancient Egypt was indissolubly bound up with her kings who had created it: they rose and fell together.

2. THE ROYAL FAMILY

The queen who had conceived the Pharaoh of the divine seed was obviously exceptionally privileged among the royal women. In all systems where the king is divine, a supernatural potential is induced in all his progeny. The eldest son of the Pharaoh by his principal consort became his heir. His eldest daughter by the same queen, the Royal heiress, was no less important since in Egypt a matriarchal system of inheritance seems to have persisted, in the Royal family at least. The dowry of the Royal heiress evidently comprised the kingdom, or perhaps the actual throne, itself an object of great sanctity as elsewhere in Africa today. It was desirable therefore in order to keep the divine essence undiluted that the Royal heir and heiress should marry each other, a full brother-sister relationship that is particularly well attested in Ptolemaic times, but for which there is no evidence among the rest of the Egyptian populace. Owing to the vagaries of infant mortality in Egypt, even among Royalty, this consummation was seldom achieved and it was often the son by a secondary wife or concubine who married the heiress, to become Crown Prince. The widow of

[1] Since earliest days, the Egyptians had held that on death they could become effective spirits (*akhu*) assuming any desired shape. In the Late Period this seems to have been modified into a belief in the transmigration of souls, as reported by Herodotus. According to this idea, the soul passed through a definite cycle of rebirth from humans through animals and back to humans again. Such a belief would fully account for the exaggerated respect, not worship, accorded to certain animals in Graeco-Roman days.

Tut-ankh-amun believed that by marrying her even a foreigner could be made a Pharaoh, and in fact her eventual second husband, the Vizier Ay who was not of Royal blood, became the next king apparently by this marriage of convenience. So powerful was the privilege that the heiress possessed of conferring the right to the throne, that Queen Hatshepsut evidently felt in the absence of full brothers on the death of her consort that she had a better right to rule than the next heir, Tuthmosis III, and was able to usurp supreme power. Though this was evidently regarded by her successors as a heresy, there are other examples of similar pretensions on the part of queens, notably by Tawosret of Dynasty XIX, and the last rulers of Dynasties VI and XII.

Occasionally, it appears, no heiress was born to or survived the king and his principal wife. This seems to have happened in the case of Amenophis III who married into a different family, perhaps a collateral branch, as did his son Amenophis IV. Yet each King subsequently consolidated his claims by marrying the first eligible heiress, his own daughter by the principal wife.

Plate 44

We are ill-informed about the careers of Royal sons, and particularly crown princes, before Dynasty XIX. It would appear that all the Royal sons received the education of a potential Pharaoh since no one could know whom fate had in store for the succession. There are several instances of heirs-apparent who did not survive their fathers. Tuthmosis III, though the son of Tuthmosis II by a secondary wife, was singled out for the kingship by the oracle of Amun. Tuthmosis IV was similarly promised the succession by Re-Harakhte. In both cases it is highly probable that no one was left with a better claim. There are occasions on which a king associated his eldest son on the throne with him as co-regent and the system is well attested for Dynasty XII. It may be that a well-regulated system of co-regency existed from the beginning, but as the Pharaohs were usually very reticent about this practice, the evidence is difficult to extract.

3 . THE HIGH OFFICIALS

In theory all government was by the king: in practice, of course, he ruled through officials. In the earliest dynasties these appear to have been his near relatives; for, since authority came from the gods, those who partook even in some small degree of the divine essence were best qualified for subordinate rule. In time, offices tended to become hereditary as the Egyptian ideal of appointing the heir to his father's place was generally followed. Veritable dynasties of officials existed by the side of the kings they served; and the genealogies of some may be traced for several generations, particularly in the New Kingdom. During the First Intermediate Period and earlier Middle Kingdom, the local governors duplicated the Royal administration on a smaller scale with their stewards, priests, and henchmen. The military State of the New Kingdom, however, was much more highly organized by a bureaucracy which is usually regarded as having no connexion with the ruling house, though the proofs are lacking. At least many of the officials had daughters in the Royal harem. No particular specialization was demanded in earlier times: thus Weni of Dynasty VI (see p. 97, above), whose training was as a steward, became in turn a judge, general, master of works, and hydraulic engineer. Ability as an organizer was apparently of more value than technical knowledge; and this remained true throughout Egyptian history. Amenophis-son-of-Hapu, for instance, whose primary office was an administrative post in the War Department, was also the architect who moved 'mountains of quartzite', as he put it, in erecting the colossal monuments of Amenophis III.

The king as the origin and fount of all law was the final

Plate 49

court of appeal. Death-sentences could apparently be con-firmed only by him and he must also have exercised prerogatives of mercy. His deputy was the vizier who was appointed or confirmed in office, together with the other high officials, at the king's advent when a traditional homily was addressed to them by the Pharaoh enjoining upon them certain principles which they were to follow, and defining their duties. The vizier was told that the responsibilities of his office were heavy, but that he was the mainstay of the entire land and must be scrupulous in administering the law, neither favouring friends, nor judging their cases more harshly because they were his friends, 'for that would be more than justice'. It has often been pointed out, however, that there is very little reference to a legal code in all this. The king was at once the legislator, judiciary, and executive, but in such a State as Egypt where the pattern of government was constantly repeated, precedent must have played a cardinal role, and a body of decisions with all the sanctity of holy writ must have been available to form the climate of Royal opinion, if not actually to affect judgements in individual cases. Even in the reign of Tuthmosis III, decisions taken by a vizier who had lived some five centuries earlier, were still recalled. There were also the *Instructions* which several kings wrote for the guidance of their posterity, and these too would form a sort of *aide-mémoire*, to give them no higher function.

In the New Kingdom an appointment perhaps of even greater importance than the post of vizier was that of the Viceroy of Ethiopia, or Prince of Kush. This official was the king's deputy in the region from el-Kab to Napata, and received the king's signet as a token of his delegated power. Though little is known about how incumbents were chosen, there is more than a suspicion that while a son of King Ahmosis may have been the first viceroy in the New Kingdom, the office soon became hereditary.

Fig. 47 The Chief of the Treasury hands over the King's signet to Huy, the Viceroy of Kush, after a painting in the tomb of Huy No. 40 at Thebes; c. 1345 B.C. Scale, 1 : 8

In the funeral procession painted in the tomb-chapel of the Vizier Ramose, we see the Prince of Kush followed by the First Herald, doubtless representing the King himself, and then the Overseer of the Treasury, a department of State as important as the judiciary. All goods and produce belonged to the Pharaoh and were distributed only by his agents. A trade in local products existed, of course, carried on from village to village on a barter system but until the Late New Kingdom, inter-State trading, like the expeditions to Punt or Byblos, was represented one-sidedly as the reception of tribute. Yet the Amarna correspondence makes it clear that the 'tribute' sent by the Pharaoh in exchange was no less valuable. The State economy was largely dependent upon the tithes collected from the land-owning institutions or individuals, whether they were large temples or veteran soldiers settled upon the land.

The taxes were in kind: barley, wheat, oil, wine, linen, fish, fruit, cattle, and so forth. The land belonged to the king and private property was created only when he made gifts. Similarly, exemptions from taxation were secured only by Royal ordinance. While land could be bequeathed to the owner's legatee, the transaction had to be ratified by Royal decree. Farm-land could apparently also be rented by tenants. A cadastre of lands was kept in the office of the vizier, and the great Wilbour Papyrus in the Brooklyn Museum shows how meticulous the land measurements and tax assessments were in Ramesside times. There is no reason to believe that they were any less precise in earlier days. A great body of officials was employed in estimating and measuring the yield of harvests and collecting, storing, and allocating the State tithes. In a State which did not have a monetary system, these taxes met the needs of the officials, craftsmen, priests, and all classes of the community not engaged upon food production.

Plate 52

4. THE ARMED FORCES

The king, as the Narmer palette makes evident, was the protector of Egypt, producing concord at home and making the State enemies his footstool abroad. His divine might alone was sufficient to conquer: in the face of his superior right, his opponents became weak and submissive. In practice, the Pharaoh was assisted in police and military matters by an army. During the later Old Kingdom, this probably consisted of local levies under their regional commanders; and it was but a short step from these to the feudal lords and their retainers that brought the miseries of civil strife to the kingdom at the collapse of Dynasty VI. There must also have been a Royal corps or bodyguard of Egyptian and Nubian troops stronger than any equivalent local force. The duties of such levies were concerned largely with police work on the frontiers,

Plate 5

Plate 36

quarrying operations in Sinai, the Wadi Hammamat, and elsewhere, and in trading expeditions to Punt. They combined the duties of a labour-corps and a protective force.

During the Middle Kingdom, the private armies of the preceding period were still tolerated until the reign of Sesostris III; and the central force of the king himself was just such a body on a larger scale, recruited by conscription but with a quota of Nubian volunteers around a nucleus of the personal retainers of the king. This army, which campaigned on a regular basis in Nubia where it also garrisoned the trading-forts, was much more highly organized than the forces of former days. Its duties still included public works and quarrying operations, besides field-service, and it was doubtless the increasing professionalism of this Army that enabled Sesostris III to suppress the last pretensions of the local barons.

The forces of the Old and Middle Kingdoms, however, have a thoroughly amateur appearance beside the large armies of the New Kingdom with their chariotry, infantry, scouts, and marines. The Theban war-lords had emerged victorious from the struggle with Hyksos and native rivals, and the character of their rule thereafter is quasi-military. Even at the Court of the unwarlike Akhenaten soldiers are prominent among the onlookers. The Army was organized into four divisions of about five thousand men each; and as this was doubtless too large a force for the population of Egypt itself to support without strain, it gradually came to be composed more and more of mercenaries—Nubians, Asiatics, Sea-peoples, and Libyans. At the Battle of Kadesh, Ramesses II had in his army a contingent of Sardinians who had been captured in previous wars; and both Nubian and Libyan prisoners could win freedom by taking service in the Pharaonic forces. A career in the Army in fact was the only opportunity for an adventurous but uneducated man, either Egyptian or alien, to achieve a position of importance or affluence. By

Plate 21

Fig. 52

enlisting as an ordinary soldier he might rise by merit to the rank of a standard-bearer, then to a company commander, and lastly to a captain of bowmen or marines. From such field-officers were chosen the police officials, sports instructors for the Royal princes, even major-domos of the princesses, and holders of other Court sinecures. Many veterans were pensioned off with grants of farm-land, valuable gold decorations, and captives as servants.

Plate 40

Plate 36

The highest staff posts in the Army, however, were open only to the educated man who might begin his career as a simple scribe acting either at home or in the field as a sort of pay-clerk. From having charge of accounts and stores, he could pass to chief army-clerk, concerned with keeping the war-diary, with reports and general secretarial work. A further elevation would be to scribe of recruits, a very important post held for example by Amenophis-son-of-Hapu, who super-intended conscription and the allocation of recruits to various services, either in the Army proper or the public works for which the Army supplied labour. The General Staff was concerned more with logistics than strategy. The Supreme Commander was the Pharaoh himself, who often delegated his authority to a deputy, usually the Crown Prince. Before a campaign the Pharaoh consulted a War Council of general officers and high State officials, though the bold and successful plan is accredited entirely to the king. The General Staff gained an unrivalled experience in the handling of large numbers of men and in organization and methods. It was perhaps for this reason that they were regarded as the best qualified to take over the kingship at different times during Dynasty XVIII, when after the deaths of Amenophis I and Tut-ankh-amun no heirs in the direct line of descent were living. Ay, Haremhab, Ramesses I, and Sethos I had all been trained as staff officers in the Army. At the end of the Ramesside period when the country was drifting into anarchy,

Plate 49

Plate 50

it was the Army officers Penhasi and Herihor who stepped in apparently to restore order: and thereafter the military secured such a hold that they were able to form a powerful caste without whose support no Pharaoh could rule, until Greek mercenaries were employed to neutralize them.

5. THE SCRIBES

For all these posts in the highly centralized administration, officials were required who could read and write; and the first necessity of any man who wished to follow a professional career was that he should be properly educated in one of the schools attached to a palace or temple where books were copied and formal instruction given. Humbler village scribes would doubtless teach their own children, and might also take a number of pupils from near relatives. The wealth of school exercises that has survived at Deir el-Medina and elsewhere suggests that the scribes found time to take advanced pupils as well as follow their calling.

If we are to judge by the career of the High Priest Bakenkhons in the reign of Ramesses II, instruction began at the age of four and was completed twelve years later. In learning the classical utterance of the Middle Kingdom, which was used for some monumental and literary purposes down to Graeco-Roman days, the pupil of a later day had to wrestle with a language which was already dead and which he understood very imperfectly as his copies of the classics clearly reveal. It is often only in such garbled forms that Egyptian literature has come down to us.

The pupil began by learning by heart the different glyphs grouped into various categories, and from that he progressed to words in the literary language selected according to meaning. From this stage he went on to copy extracts from the classics, sometimes translating them into the vernacular language.

Papyrus was too expensive for beginners to spoil and potsherds and flakes of limestone (*ostraka*) had to serve instead. The instruction in reading and writing comprised other subjects as well. The writing of the various glyphs demanded an ability to draw with the pen. Geography, mathematics, foreign words, articles of trade, travelling equipment, religious feasts, parts of the body, and so forth, were learnt incidentally in copying stock-letters, poems on the King and his Residences, and the various exchanges in a literary controversy between two learned scribes. Learning without tears may have been the ideal in some respects, although the Egyptians also had a Tudor belief in the efficacy of corporal punishment and the pupil was told that if he was idle he would be soundly thrashed. It is not surprising that under such treatment, and obsessed with the tedium of learning, the schoolboy should have thought of running away to become a soldier or charioteer or farmer; and repeatedly by means of such homilies as *The Satire on Trades* the teacher sought to make his pupils stick to their dull tasks, comparing the easy lot of the trained scribe with the miseries of other callings. The theme is usually that the profession of scribe leads to a comfortable well-paid job: but some hint of the pleasure of learning for its own sake is given in the injunction to 'acquire this high calling of scribe; pleasant and fruitful are your pen and papyrus roll, and happy are you the livelong day'. There is evidence that some girls were taught to read and write, for profit as well as pleasure. A word for a female scribe exists by the time of the Middle Kingdom at least, and a more emphatic expression is current in the Late Period. Writing-palettes of two of Akenaten's daughters have survived and there is a graffito in the Step Pyramid with a sneering reference to the literary efforts of women.

When the scribe had graduated from school he had his foot on the first rung of a career in the higher ranks of the Army, the Treasury, or the Palace. He might become anything

Plate 62

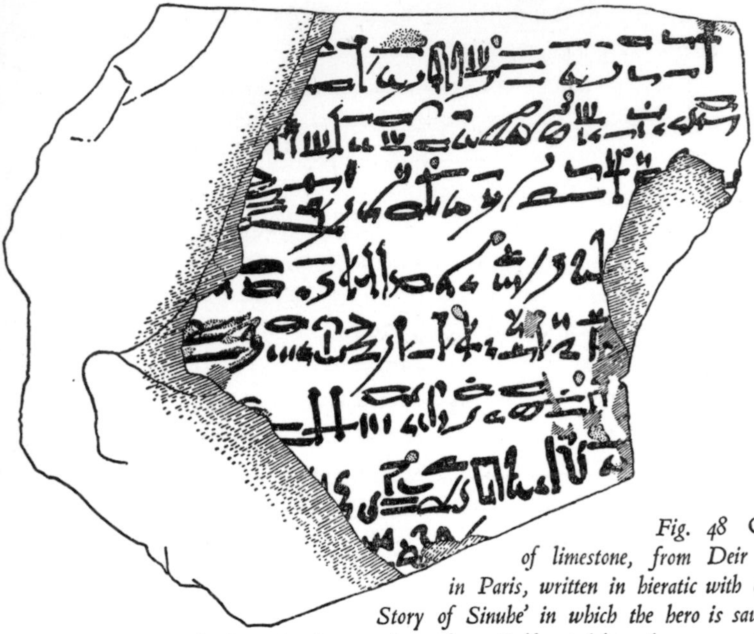

Fig. 48 Ostrakon, or flake of limestone, from Deir el-Medina and now in Paris, written in hieratic with a passage from 'The Story of Sinuhe' in which the hero is saved by Bedouin from death in the desert and travels to Byblos and beyond; c. 1150 B.C. Length 7½ in.

according to his talents, from the king's private secretary to the village letter-writer and petty attorney. It would help, of course, if he could follow his father in his chosen occupation, but occasionally a man from humble circumstances was able to rise by merit to a position of authority. Some of the high officers of State during the New Kingdom boast of their lowly birth, and though in most cases they exaggerate in order to flatter the king who had advanced them, nevertheless such a factotum as Sennemut did come from modest antecedents, his father having only a vague, and probably posthumous, title of 'worthy'.

A training as a scribe was also a necessary preliminary to a career in such professions as medicine, the priesthood, and art and architecture. A medical student would be apprenticed to

Plate 40

a practitioner, almost always his father or some near relative; but an ability to read was necessary for learning the various prescriptions, spells, and diagnoses contained in medical papyri, whether the work in question were a quasi-scientific treatise on surgery and fractures such as the Edwin Smith Papyrus, or a specialist work on gynaecology such as the Kahun Papyrus, or a mere collection of medico-magic recipes, nostrums, and incantations such as the Ebers Papyrus.

During the Old and Middle Kingdoms the priesthood had been a largely amateur organization, the district worthy being the chief priest *ex officio* of the local god, though he may have been assisted by a number of full-time subordinate priests. During the New Kingdom, however, with the considerable resources that were lavished upon such State gods as Amun of Thebes, Ptah of Memphis, and Re-Harakhte of Heliopolis, the priesthood became a highly specialized profession. The chief priests are great secular administrators as well as ecclesi-astics. Thus Amun had not only four prophets or high priests, Plates 67, 53 and a host of minor officiants down to bearers of floral offerings, but a complete secular establishment, a Chief Steward and Overseers of his Granary, Store-houses, Cattle, Huntsmen, Peasants, Weavers, Craftsmen, Goldsmiths, Sculptors, Ship-wrights, Draughtsmen, Records, and Police, a veritable enclave within the Pharaonic State. All these posts and their subordinate offices had to be filled with trained scribes, though the degree of their proficiency naturally varied.

It is more difficult to determine whether the training of a scribe was demanded of artists and craftsmen who are so Fig. 15 largely represented as working anonymously in studios attached to the palaces and temples. It is clear that sculptors and painters need not have been able to read or write so long as they could copy on a large scale what was drawn on an *ostrakon* or papyrus by a master-scribe or draughtsman. Models of hiero-glyphs were supplied in plaster for ignorant workmen to copy at Amarna, and there is plenty of evidence from this same site that stock subjects and texts were copied mechanically from year to year even when they were out of date, and if corrected at all, only after they had been cut into the stone. During the Middle Kingdom many *ex votos* were mass-produced at Abydos, for instance, by craftsmen who could not write, the inscription usually being feebly scratched on by a hand more used to wielding a pen than a chisel. From this and other evidence it is usually argued that the artist was of little account, a despised and humble workman devilling away for a literate official who took all the credit. Such judgements, however, ignore the essentially objective approach of the ancient craftsman to his work. It is inconceivable that the Ancient Egyptians, who were the most artistic nation of the Ancient World and of whom it may justly be said that nothing they touched they did not adorn, should not have valued high artistic skill. There is a suggestion in a text that Tuthmosis III may have designed stone vessels, and it seems almost certain that the extraordinary mannerism of Amarna art can only have originated in the imagination of Akhenaten himself. The fact is that especially in the earlier periods it was seldom that artists proclaimed their calling: they preferred to masquerade under such titles as the High Priest of Ptah. Several Court artists were given handsome tombs at Thebes by their grateful sovereigns. Parennefer was honoured by a tomb at Amarna as well as at Thebes where he is prouder of his title of the king's cupbearer than that of chief craftsman of the king. In his interesting biography, the king's architect Nekhebu of Dynasty VI mentions only incidentally the fact that he began

Plate 46
Fig. 4

cf. Plate 71

Fig. 49   Yuti, the chief sculptor of Queen Tiy (see Plate 44), putting the finishing touches to a statuette of her daughter Beket-aten; after a relief in the tomb of Huya at Amarna; c. 1357 B.C. Scale, 1 : 4

his career by acting as secretary to his brother, an Overseer of Works; and the evidence that he had received the training of a scribe is missing from the list of his many titles.

6. PEASANTS AND WORKERS

The cleavage between the scribal *élite* and the uneducated masses was wide and deep. Several sages exhort their posterity not to be arrogant because of their knowledge. The Vizier Ptah-hotep claims that a good discourse is rarer than precious stone, yet it is found with serving-girls at the mill-stones. But too often, especially with the petty official, the view prevailed that the scribe existed to drive the ignorant man like a pack-ass. The liability of the common man to be directed by his betters is seen in the operation of the *corvée*, a system which had existed from earliest days whereby all the able-bodied men could be called out in critical times as during the harvest and inundation to toil on public works such as the raising of dykes or the clearing of channels to control the flood. Unskilled labour was also conscripted to accompany remote quarrying expeditions. A similar impress was doubtless employed for hauling cut stone in the building of the pyramids, probably during the inundation when the peasantry were largely un-employed. That any considerable body of rural labour could have been withdrawn permanently from the fields without endangering the economy of the country is extremely im-probable. The dragomans' stories of the building of the Giza pyramids, current by the time Herodotus visited them, and the biased Biblical accounts of Israel in bondage, have promoted the popular idea that Ancient Egypt was inhabited by an oppressed people toiling under privileged task-masters. The impression we get from the monuments is altogether different. It did happen sometimes that men were pushed too hard and had to obtain redress by appealing to higher authority or in

cf. Plate 61

extreme cases by leaving the cultivation of their fields. We also have details of workers' strikes in Ramesside times when through mismanagement their pay fell into arrears. But these cases were exceptional. The ideal impressed by the sages in their teachings was that the official should act considerately towards the weak and defenceless man. 'If a poor cultivator is in arrears with his taxes, remit two-thirds of them', was the advice of one. That the basic wealth of Egypt was in its agriculture was well understood at all times when the magnates took pleasure in representing themselves absorbed in country life, in the work of gardens and vineyards as well as fields and stockyards. The picture may be idealized, but the rural life which they wished to perpetuate was regarded as the perfect one. We see the peasant busy in the fields at the seasons of sowing or reaping, though even then he has a chance to snooze during the midday break, or take a pull at a convenient wine-skin, and we realize that what was required of him was hard work in short bursts. During the inundation, when the country became a vast lake with the towns standing up above the waters on their mounds, there was a chance for relaxing, though the cattle then had to be fed by hand. There were also feast-days when it was not propitious to work: and always the peasant had the time and spirit to sing his work-songs as he drove his team round the threshing-floor, or carried the calf across the ford where the fishes and crocodile lurked. This rural life is attractively revealed as a busy one yet full of dignity and inward peace in *The Tale of the Two Brothers*, where the hero is a simple peasant lad who toils daily in his brother's fields. Sowing and reaping were duties that even the highest in the land expected to discharge in the fields of the Osirian other-world where the wheat stood nine cubits high, though the shawabti-figure would undertake the more onerous tasks of the *corvée*. In *The Satire on Trades* the scribe gives a highly coloured account of the farmer contending with drought, locusts, mice,

Plates 18, 52
Figs. 11, 12, 32

Plate 52

Fig. 50   The village headman receiving a supply of seed-corn from the clerk to the Keeper of the Storeroom, sowing the irrigated land, and turning in the seed with a shallow plough drawn by two cows; from a relief in a tomb near el-Bersha; c. 2330 B.C. Scale, 1 : 11

thieves, and the tax-collector: yet to the Greek, used to bitter toil on his own arid hills and stony pastures, Egypt seemed a lush land where crops grew with little effort. Each year the inundation deposited a rich silt over the old fields on which it was only necessary to scatter the grain and turn it in with a shallow plough drawn by a pair of cows. A main crop and a smaller summer crop could be harvested each year, the labour being largely concerned with the basin system of irrigation, raising dykes, cutting channels to let water flow from one level to another, and using the well-sweep or *shadūf* in summer to water the fields.

A less independent life would appear to have been led by the minor craftsmen and unskilled labourers in the towns. The ruins of their quarters have come to light at Thebes, Amarna, and Lahun where they lived in houses, usually of two or three rooms, within a walled enclosure. They were dependent for their rations upon the labour of others and if the commissariat failed or was venal they went hungry. Yet it would be wrong to draw conclusions from exceptional circumstances when the system broke down. Compared with the bathrooms, privies, loggias, bedrooms, halls, and store-rooms of the wealthy, their living-quarters may appear cramped but were no worse than the hovel of the peasant who often lived with his beasts. We

Plate 43

Fig. 51 An annual distribution of clothing and oils to Syrian slave-women and their children attached to the temple of Amun at Karnak, after a painting in the tomb of the Vizier Rekhmire, No. 100 at Thebes; c. 1440 B.C. Scale, 1 : 6

shall, in fact, be extremely well equipped to get a picture of the life of the worker in Ancient Egypt more detailed and intimate than that of any other nation of Antiquity, or indeed of modern times, when Professor Černý of Oxford has completed his study of the great mass of records from Deir el-Medina. Here for nearly four centuries at Thebes lived generations of the workers employed mostly on tombs of the Pharaohs in the near-by Valley of the Kings—stone-masons, painters, draughts-men, scribes, metal-workers, sculptors, artisans of all kinds

Plate 61

together with their labourers and auxiliaries. They were
inveterate scribblers and from different sites at Thebes thousands
of *ostraka* and some papyri have been recovered on which they
jotted accounts, rosters, progress reports, work-sheets, provisions,
testaments, sketches, and records of every kind. Already the
life of this long-dead community is beginning to emerge as
the material is sorted and studied. We know that the artisans
were divided into shifts each under a foreman, that families
intermarried, sons usually taking their father's posts except
when influence had been used to get someone else appointed.
Absenteeism was common, the excuses being many and
various. Workmen did not report for duty when their wives
were menstruating, probably because they then became ritually
impure. We know the scale of rations provided and the extent
of an average day's stint. An examination of the 'lamp account',
and the daily issue of wicks, has cast light of a different sort on
the length of the working day which will come as a surprise
to those who think the life of the ancient worker was one of
unremitting toil.

It may, however, be properly argued that the workmen of
Deir el-Medina were skilled craftsmen some of them wealthy
enough to have handsomely decorated tombs of their own.
The lowest grade in the social scale was occupied by the serfs.
Like all other nations of Antiquity, Egypt employed slave-
labour. Captives taken in war were doubtless regarded as
second-class citizens from earliest times, though the evidence
does not begin to accumulate before the Middle Kingdom
when, as we have seen, both Nubians and Asiatics took service
in Egypt, either being sold into slavery, or exchanging a
penurious and uncertain freedom for security and a modest
subsistence. We have also seen how some such serfs were able
to attain positions of trust and importance, and doubtless to
secure their independence. Slavery on a greater scale existed
during the New Kingdom when foreign wars and ethnic

Fig. 48
Plate 62

Plate 53

Fig. 52   A Syrian mercenary with his wife drinks beer through a reed, with an Egyptian servant in attendance; after a stela from Amarna, now in Berlin; c. 1355 B.C. Scale, 1:2

movements brought a lot of prisoners and refugees into the Nile Valley. We find captives assigned as serfs to the temples and private estates, and even to the household of Army officers. But the demarcation between slave and citizen was fluid. The personal slave of a high-ranking Egyptian would be far more affluent than most of the native peasantry. By Ramesside times foreigners held important posts in the Palace and the Army. A stela from earlier Amarna days shows a Syrian mercenary being waited upon by a native Egyptian. While slaves could be bought and sold or hired out, the Wilbour Papyrus makes it clear that they could also rent and cultivate land on the same conditions as an Army officer, priest, or other official. A simple declaration by the owner before witnesses was apparently sufficient to make a slave into a 'freedman of the land of Pharaoh', and one document has survived in which a woman adopted as her heirs the offspring of her dead husband and a female slave they had purchased, in preference to nearer relatives. Another case exists of a barber who married his orphan niece to a slave to whom he bequeathed his business.

The most wretched of Pharaoh's subjects were the criminals, some of them officials who had been found guilty of corruption; they were banished to the lonely frontier fortress of Tjel, or forced to labour in the mines of Sinai and Nubia, often after losing their noses.

CHAPTER X
The Egyptian Way of Life

IN THE FOREGOING chapters we have incidentally plotted the rough shape of the ideology that determined the character of the Ancient Egyptian civilization. No understanding of the Ancient Egyptians, however, can be complete without a far more detailed study of their complex religious beliefs than is possible here, and we must content ourselves with strengthening the outline at one or two salient points.

Most scholars who have studied Ancient Egyptian religion have subjected it to a modern theological examination and systematic analysis outside of its context that it is not fitted by nature to endure. The result has been an exposure of confused and conflicting concepts intractable to the logical processes brought to bear upon them. For the Egyptian view of reality was achieved through what the late Henri Frankfort, the most acute and sympathetic of interpreters, has defined as a 'multiplicity of approaches', in contrast to the one unified and coherent theory which is the child of Greek thought. To a single consistent simile, the Egyptian opposed a number of mixed metaphors arising from an exuberance of images perceived through the imagination.

In shaping his habits of thought, his environment must have played a decisive part. Egypt is a land of antitheses: all around there are startling contrasts, none more compelling than the distinction between the black cultivation and the red desert, between a teeming fecund life and the most sterile death. It is not perhaps surprising that the Egyptian should have conceived of his world as a duality of opposites maintained in even balance. He felt mental discomfort, or the presence of evil, whenever this equilibrium was upset. His need to establish equipoise is seen in the symmetry of his art and architecture, in the balanced parallelisms of his more dignified utterances, in the creation of the political duality of the 'Two Lands', above all in his conception of *ma'at* (see p. 161, above).

Egypt provided a physical *milieu* in which this balance could be easily secured, for its natural conditions are almost changeless. It escapes the earthquakes that devastate from time to time the Aegean world. It has climate but no weather. Each day the sun rises in glory, traverses the heavens unobscured, and sets in splendour. Each year the Nile rises with predictable regularity and rejuvenates the tired land: only the volume of its inundation remains uncertain. Until the Late Period, the desert margins protected the Egyptians from those wayward floods of invaders that have altered radically the history and fates of other ancient peoples. The infiltration of new races with new ideas was gradual enough to ensure that the native culture would be irrigated, not swamped, by such contacts. This environment fostered the Egyptian instinct to maintain a *status quo*. The dry sands have preserved much of the ancient past as a dominant present. Perhaps it is not wholly fortuitous that Egypt should be the traditional land of mummification.

In such stable conditions the Egyptian view of the cosmos is essentially static: change is only a recurring rhythm, not a progression. The struggle between the opposing forces is evenly matched. The land may be parched in summer, but the inundation will come. The old king Osiris will suffer death, but his son the new Horus will reign in his stead. The victory of the sun-god is proclaimed with every dawn, though his death will occur at dusk. The Egyptians had no cosmogony to teach them that in the beginning man had fallen by defying God; or that he had once lived in a Golden Age from which he had declined. Still less was there any idea of progress towards a fuller material existence on earth. Government had come from the gods who had ruled Egypt from the moment of its creation. It was, therefore, perfect at its inception, and

since it was still in the hands of a god, incapable of improve-
ment.

> Well tended are men, the cattle of God. He made heaven
> and earth according to their desire. He allayed their thirst [?]
> He made the air to bring life to their nostrils. They are his
> images that have gone forth from his limbs. . . . But he also
> slew his enemies.[1]

So wrote the father of King Mery-ka-re (see p. 105, above),
referring also to an ancient myth that taught that the sun-god
decided to punish men for their insolence, but in the end took
pity on them and relented. The view of the Egyptian was that
though it was in the nature of man to transgress, yet it was in
the nature of gods to forgive, for their 'wrath is finished in a
moment'. There is thus a complete lack of any sense of guilt
in the Egyptian psyche: and that fundamental unease which
has given so much of mankind a motive force either for good
or ill, was replaced in the Egyptian by another compulsion,
the need not to put himself right with God, but to attune
himself to the system of *ma'at* which had been created by God.

By nature he lived secure from most of the worries that
beset neighbouring peoples, and he had further fortified himself against anxiety by accepting the rule of a god incarnate.
All this was in accord with his static but joyous reception of
the world as it was, created by the gods perfect and evenly
balanced, 'alive from end to end'. The evidence is implicit in
his art where, if the magnate is represented in all his finery
calmly surveying the work of his fields, then the shambling,
unkempt rustic at his menial tasks must also appear to complete the antithesis. The dignity of the high official and his
family is counterbalanced by the undisciplined behaviour of
the gleaners squabbling over the corn-ears. While the fisherman
is in the marshes, the marauding ichneumon seeks the nest of

[1] After Erman-Blackman: *Literature*, p. 83.

the water-fowl. If the hunter is in the desert, then the hyena pounces upon the newly dropped kid. We explain all this teeming incident as due to the artist's keen and humorous delight in the world around him. It is also due to something more instinctive—a feeling that without its antithetical corre-lates, his universe is out of balance.

The equipoise of the Egyptian world was *ma'at*, which may have the meaning of 'order', 'truth', 'justice', according to its context. It was achieved whenever the natural harmony of the cosmos existing at the moment of its creation, was restored after a period of discord. Such disorder, or falsehood, or injustice, occurred most notably during the First Intermediate Period when the times got out of joint, the established order was destroyed by anarchy, and life no longer had meaning. Similar chaos or anti-*ma'at* occurred between the death of the god-ruler and the coronation of his successor. Such crises were only dispelled with the re-establishment of *ma'at*, and it is significant that in coronation-scenes the Pharaoh is frequently shown accompanied by the goddess who personifies *Ma'at*. Thus the joy and release from tension on the accession of Merenptah is expressed by one poet in the following words:

> *Ma'at* has overcome falsehood, the transgressors are over-thrown, the greedy are repulsed. The water stands and fails not, and the Nile carries a high flood. The days are long, the nights have hours and the months come aright. The gods are content and light of heart, and life is spent in laughter and wonder.[1]

For the Egyptian, the good life consisted in achieving *ma'at*. 'Truth is good and its worth is lasting and it has not been disturbed since the day of its creator', wrote Ptah-hotep for his son. 'He who transgresses its ordinances is punished. It lies as a right path in front of even the ignorant.' This ignorance

[1] After Erman-Blackman: *Literature*, p. 278.

could be dispelled by knowledge, [for the Egyptian believed
that though a proper attitude to life was not easy to attain, it
could be taught like any branch of his learning, and the books
of instruction that have come down to us, nearly all garbled as
school exercises, hold up the ideals to be achieved. A number
of prayers written by men who believed they had offended a
god, but in which they confess that they had been ignorant,
not wicked, have also survived. 'Punish me not for my many
misdeeds', wrote one. 'I am one who knows not himself [?].
I am a witless man. All day long I follow my mouth like an
ox after fodder.']

Such men are described in the 'teachings' as 'passionate'
men who are doomed to unhappiness and ultimate failure
because they are arrogant, greedy, and contentious. Such men
are unlucky and best avoided. Their counterpart is the 'tranquil'
man who is content with his lot, modest, patient, and bene-
volent. Only such a man is successful because he does not
destroy the harmony that exists in the cosmos but becomes
part of it. If the Egyptian did wrong, therefore, it was objectively
against the divine system of *ma'at*, not by a subjective conflict
between himself and a supreme god who was usually too
remote anyway and only approachable through the intermediary
of the divine king or some local godling.

The upheavals of the Late Period with its dynastic tensions,
its failures abroad, the subjugation of its Pharaohs by foreign
conquerors, and the eclipse of the national fortunes, dealt the
idea of *ma'at* an even more grievous blow than it had suffered
during the upheavals of the First Intermediate Period. The
best the Egyptian could do was to hark back to a past when
men, it seemed, had been able to establish a harmony within
their world. By repeating their outward and visible signs it
was thought that their inward and spiritual grace would also
be achieved; but it was in vain. The Egyptians, like all such
pre-scientific peoples, had been directed largely by magic,

which in its earlier days had worked for a beneficent end, giving confidence and discipline to her people and enabling the odds of adversity to be overcome. It achieved results because it did not encroach upon the domain of empirical knowledge. Thus every year ceremonies were performed to ensure that the Nile rose; yet these rites were not observed except at the season of inundation. In the destruction of the old confidence in the face of constant adversity during the Late Period, the Egyptians came more and more to rely upon supernatural intervention, upon oracles, horoscopes, spells, amulets, and all the apparatus of magic that earned the contempt of Isaiah and the bewilderment of Greek and Roman. We should, however, judge the Ancient Egyptians not from the nervous breakdown of their old age, but from what they were during the two thousand years when their system worked and, in the words of Frankfort, 'the life of man, as an individual and even more as a member of society, was integrated with the life of nature, and . . . the experience of that harmony was thought to be the greatest good to which man could aspire'.[1]

[1] H. Frankfort: *Religion*, p. 29.

Select Bibliography

CHAPTER I

DAWSON, WARREN R., *Who was Who in Egyptology*, London, 1951.
GLANVILLE, S. R. K., *The Growth and Nature of Egyptology*, Cambridge, 1947.
MONTET, PIERRE, *Isis, ou à la recherche de l'Égypte ensevelie*, Paris, 1956.
PETRIE, W. M. F., *Seventy Years in Archaeology*, London, 1931.

CHAPTER II

BAIKIE, JAMES, *Egyptian Antiquities in the Nile Valley, A Descriptive Handbook*, London, 1932.
CAPART, JEAN et WERBROUCK, MARCELLE, *Thebes, The Glory of a Great Past*, London, 1926.
CAPART, JEAN et WERBROUCK, MARCELLE, *Memphis à l'Ombre des Pyramides*, Bruxelles, 1930.
PENDLEBURY, J. D. S., *Tell el-Amarna*, London, 1935.

CHAPTER III

CLARKE, SOMERS and ENGELBACH, R., *Ancient Egyptian Masonry*, London, 1930.
KEES, HERMANN, 'Ägypten' (*Handbuch der Altertumswissenschaft III*, pt. 1, *No. 3*), Munich, 1933.
LUCAS, A., *Ancient Egyptian Materials and Industries*, 3rd ed., London, 1948.
MONTET, PIERRE (trans. by A. R. Maxwell-Hyslop and Margaret S. Drower), *Everyday Life in Egypt*, London, 1958.
WADDELL, W. G. (ed.), *Herodotus*, Book II, London, 1939.

CHAPTERS IV–VIII

*DRIOTON, ÉTIENNE et VANDIER, JACQUES, 'L'Égypte' (*Les Peuples de L'Orient Méditerranéen, II*), 3rd ed. revised, Paris, 1952.
ERMAN, ADOLF (trans. by Aylward M. Blackman), *The Literature of the Ancient Egyptians*, London, 1927.

*HAYES, WILLIAM C., *The Sceptre of Egypt*, Parts I and II, New York, 1953 and 1959.

SMITH, W. STEVENSON, *Art and Architecture of Ancient Egypt*, London, 1958.

WILSON, JOHN A., 'Egyptian Texts' in PRITCHARD, JAMES B. (ed.), *Ancient Near Eastern Texts Relating to the Old Testament*, Princeton, 1950.

CHAPTERS IV and V

DAVIES, N. de G., *The Mastaba of Ptahhetep and Akhethetep*, Parts I and II, London, 1900–1.

DUELL, PRENTICE, *The Mastaba of Mereruka*, Vols. I and II, Chicago, 1938.

EDWARDS, I. E. S., *The Pyramids of Egypt* (Revised ed.), London, 1960.

FRANKFORT, HENRI, *The Birth of Civilisation in the Near East*, London, 1951.

VANDIER, J., *Manuel d'Archéologie Égyptienne*, Vols. I and II, Paris, 1952–5.

CHAPTER VI

BLACKMAN, AYLWARD M., *The Rock Tombs of Meir*, Parts I–VI, London, 1914–53.

POSENER, G., *Littérature et Politique dans L'Égypte de la XIIe Dynastie*, Paris, 1956.

SÄVE-SÖDERBERGH, T., 'The Hyksos Rule in Egypt' (*Journal of Egyptian Archaeology*, XXXVII, 1951, pp. 53–71).

WINLOCK, H. E., *The Rise and Fall of the Middle Kingdom in Thebes*, New York, 1947.

WINLOCK, H. E., *The Treasure of el Lahun*, New York, 1934.

WINLOCK, H. E., *Models of Daily Life in Ancient Egypt*, Cambridge, Mass., 1955.

CHAPTERS VII and VIII

DAVIES, NINA DE GARIS and GARDINER, ALAN H., *The Tomb of Amenemhet*, London, 1915.

DAVIES, NORMAN DE GARIS, *Two Ramesside Tombs at Thebes*, New York, 1927.

ELGOOD, P. G., *The Later Dynasties of Egypt*, Oxford, 1951.

FOX, PENELOPE, *Tutankhamun's Treasure*, London, 1951.

GURNEY, O. R., *The Hittites*, London, 1952.

STEINDORFF, GEORGE and SEELE, KEITH C., *When Egypt Ruled the East*, 2nd ed., Chicago, 1957.

WINLOCK, H. E., *Excavations at Deir el-Bahri*, 1911–31, New York, 1942.

CHAPTER IX

FAULKNER, R. O., 'Egyptian Military Organisation' (*Journal of Egyptian Archaeology*, XXXVII, 1951, pp. 53–71).

FRANKFORT, HENRI, *Kingship and the Gods*, Chicago, 1948.

WAINWRIGHT, G. A., *The Sky-Religion in Egypt*, Cambridge, 1938.

CHAPTER X

ČERNÝ, JAROSLAV, *Ancient Egyptian Religion*, London, 1952.

FRANKFORT, HENRI, *Ancient Egyptian Religion, an Interpretation*, New York, 1948.

WILSON, JOHN A., *The Burden of Egypt, an Interpretation of Ancient Egyptian Culture*, Chicago, 1951.

* The works marked with an asterisk have extensive bibliographies to which the reader is referred for more advanced study.

Sources of Illustrations

Acknowledgement is made to the following for their courtesy in supply-
ing photographs and drawings, from which the illustrations have been
made, and for permission to publish them: Mr George W. Allan,
London: Pl. 1, 6, 25, 38, 56, 57, 82; Service des Antiquités, Cairo:
Pl. 16, 17, 24, 26, 30, 36, 67, Fig. 11; Berlin Museum, Pl. 45; Museum
of Fine Arts, Boston: Pl. 8, 10, 12, 64–6; Mr Bernard V. Bothmer,
Brooklyn: Pl. 31, 77, 80; The Trustees of the British Museum, London:
Pl. 22, 40, Fig. 23; Brooklyn Museum: Pl. 13, 20, 29, 42, 78, 79, 81;
Oriental Institute, University of Chicago: Pl. 18, 35, 51, 52, 59, 60, Fig.
22, 32, 33, 41; Egypt Exploration Society, London: Pl. 43, 54, Fig. 3,
14, 20, 39, 43, 44, 46, 48, 50; Eton College, Windsor: Pl. 68; The
Syndics of the Fitzwilliam Museum, Cambridge: Pl. 58; Mr John
R. Freeman, London: Pl. 19; Photo-Wehmeyer, Hildesheim: Pl.
11; Professor Max Hirmer, Munich: Pl. 7, 15, 23, 46, 49; Institut
Français, Cairo: Fig. 10, 12; Dr Kurt Lange, Oberstdorf: Pl. 5; Louvre,
Paris: Pl. 2, 63, 71; Metropolitan Museum of Art, New York: Pl. 3, 4,
14, 27, 39, 47, 50, 53, 61, 70, and Pl. 9, 21, 33, 41, 44, 48, 55,
based on photographs by Mr Harry Burton, Fig. 15, 51; Professor Pierre
Montet, Paris: Pl. 69; Professor H. W. Müller, Munich: Pl. 73, 74, 76;
Royal Scottish Museum, Edinburgh: Pl. 32, 34, 72, 75; Mr and Mrs
Robert J. Sainsbury, London: Pl. 28; Dr C. T. Trechmann, Castle
Eden: jacket-cover; Turin Museum: Pl. 62; Martin E. Weaver, London:
Fig. 29, 30 (after Borchardt); Thames and Hudson: Fig. 40 (after
Naville); H. A. Shelley: Fig. 2, 8.
The following drawings have been made by the author: Fig. 4 (after
Davies), 5–7, 9, 13 (after Davies), 16–19, 21, 24 (after Quibell), 25
(after Gardiner-Peet), 26–8, 31, 34 (after Petrie), 35–8, 42, 45, 47 and
49 (after Davies), 52.

2

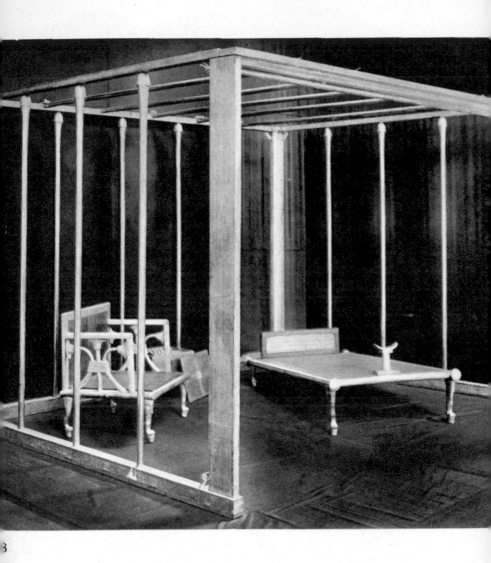

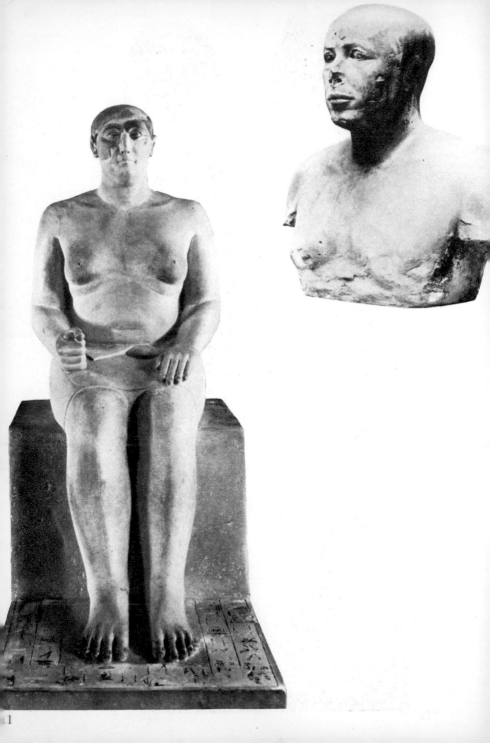

12

13   14

16

23   24

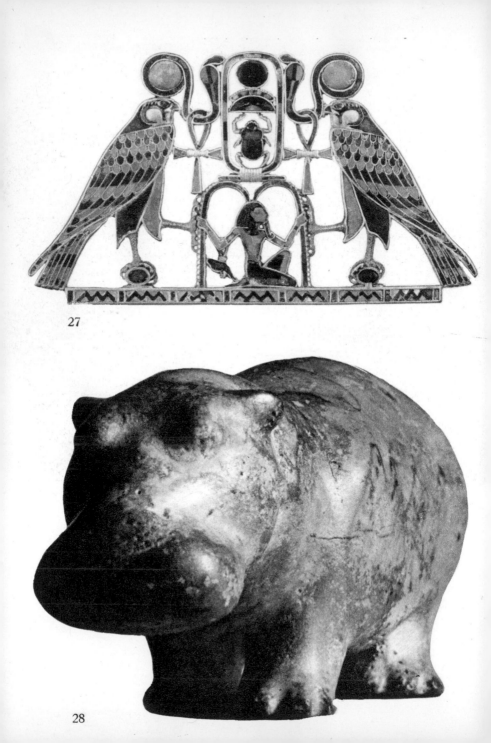

27

28

30

31

32

4

40

43

44   45

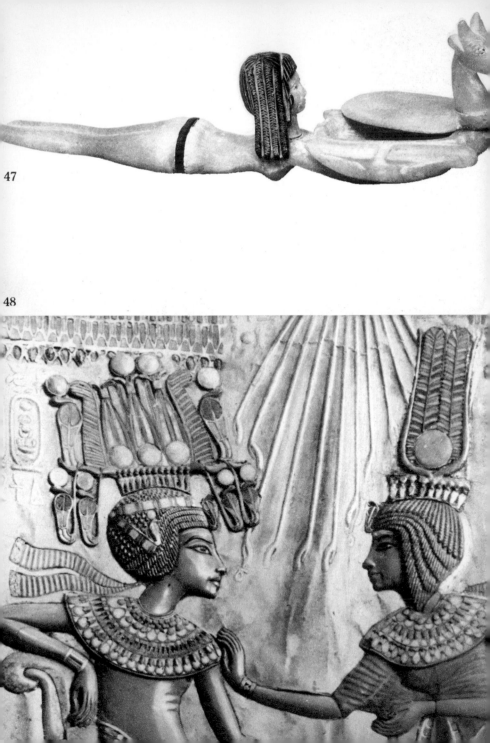

47

48

49

50

51

58

61

62

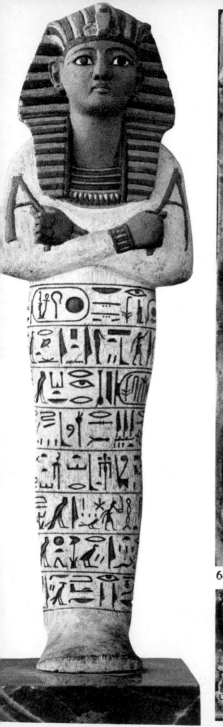

64

65

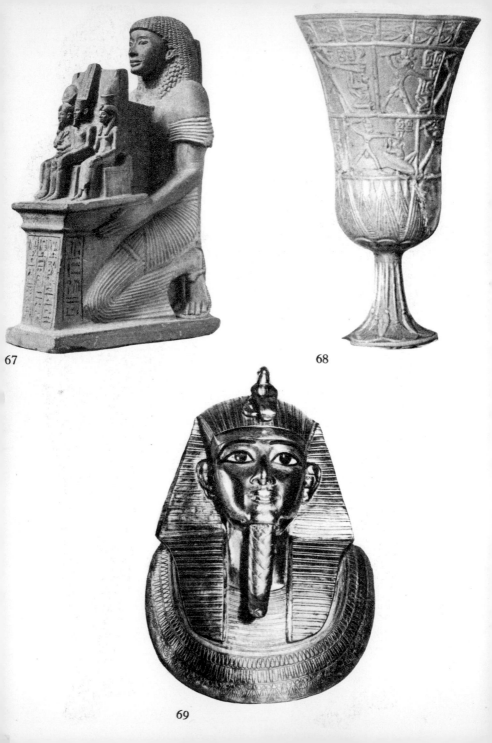

67

68

69

70   71

72

73

74

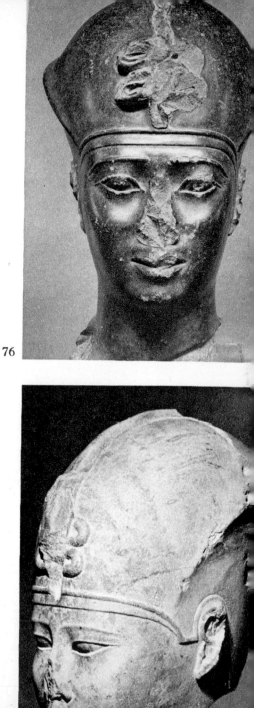

76

77

Notes on the Plates

1. The Nile at the Island of Elephantine, the traditional southern frontier and the seat of powerful governors who kept the border with Nubia during the Old Kingdom. Near here were famous granite quarries. Temples of Tuthmosis III and Amenophis III, which were still standing when the French Expedition recorded them in 1802, have since been demolished.

2. Predynastic flint knife with ivory handle carved on both sides with scenes of warfare and the chase. On the side illustrated are disposed figures of two different warrior groups in combat, slain foemen, and ships of foreign as well as native type. From Gebel el-Arak, south of Abydos. Height 11 in. The Louvre, Paris.

3. Spouted libation bowl, with compartments formed by two hieroglyphs, carved out of slate. The form has been inspired by a metal prototype. Archaic Period, c. 3000 B.C. Length 7 in. Metropolitan Museum, New York.

4. Ivory supports for beds or stools and gaming boards, carved as the fore and rear legs of bulls. From Abydos. Archaic Period, c. 3000 B.C. Height $2\frac{1}{2}$ to $6\frac{1}{2}$ in. Metropolitan Museum, New York.

5. Votive slate palette of King Narmer (reverse) showing the Pharaoh wearing the White Crown of Upper Egypt and sacrificing a foe. On the obverse, Narmer, wearing the Red Crown of Lower Egypt inspects the bodies of slain rebels at Buto (?) and in the guise of a strong bull breaks into an enemy stronghold and tramples a Libyan (?) underfoot. Excavated at Hierakonpolis by J. E. Quibell working for Flinders Petrie. Dynasty I, c. 3200 B.C. Length 26 in. Cairo Museum.

6. The Step Pyramid of King Djoser at Saqqara showing the main structure and fluted engaged columns in a subsidiary building partly restored. In

this great monument, Imhotep, the King's architect, introduced a completely new form, the stepped mastaba, for the royal tomb which previously had not differed in conception from those of private persons. Dynasty III, *c.* 2650 B.C.

7 Limestone panel, one of three carved in relief in niches framed with blue faience tiles in a gallery under a subsidiary mastaba within the Step Pyramid complex. The scene shows the King wearing the White Crown of the South and carrying the *ladanisterion* as he runs along a circuit between hoof-shaped boundary marks probably symbolizing the territories over which he ruled. Above him hovers the protective hawk-god, Horus of Edfu (*cf.* Plate 82), carrying the symbol of life. Dynasty III, *c.* 2650 B.C. Height 37 in.

8 Gold-sheathed wood furniture of Queen Hetep-heres, consisting of a portable canopy (height 86 in.) from which fine curtains like a mosquito net were originally hung, and which bears the name and titles of her husband King Sneferu. Also in this group are a chair, jewel-box, and bed with headrest and inlaid footboard, some of them the gift of her son Kheops. The original woodwork had decayed to the condition of cigar-ash and has been restored by the excavators. From Giza. Dynasty IV, *c.* 2590 and 2575 B.C. Cairo Museum.

9 Detail from a seated statue of King Khephren a little over life-size, in grey-green diorite showing the King under the protection of the hawk-god Horus. This statue escaped the destruction of some hundred similar sculptures from the King's pyramid complex through being cast down a pit in the Valley Temple (Fig. 28) where it was found by Mariette in 1853. From Giza. Dynasty IV, *c.* 2520 B.C. Cairo Museum.

10 Painted limestone bust of the Prince and Vizier Ankh-haf, with the surfaces modelled in a skin of plaster. From Giza. Dynasty IV, *c.* 2525 B.C. Height 20 in. Museum of Fine Arts, Boston.

11 Limestone statue of the Prince and Vizier Hemon. Like the contemporary 'reserve heads' (Fig. 31) the surfaces are unpainted, but the inscription is inlaid in coloured pastes in the traditions of the reign of Sneferu,

whose son Hemon was. From Giza. Dynasty IV, *c.* 2550 B.C. Height 62 in. Pelizaeus Museum, Hildesheim.

12 Dark slate pair-statue of King Mykerinus and his Queen. The statue is complete, but the lower part lacks the polish that has been imparted to the features: with the Khephren of Plate 9, one of the supreme masterpieces of royal sculpture in Egypt. From Giza. Dynasty IV, *c.* 2500 B.C. Height 56 in. Museum of Fine Arts, Boston.

13 Limestone group-statue of the Overseer of the Granary Iruka-Ptah, his wife and son. The composition with the woman on a much smaller scale kneeling at her husband's feet is known from a fragmentary statue of Kheops' successor. From Saqqara. Late Dynasty V, *c.* 2370 B.C. Height 29 in. Brooklyn Museum.

14 Limestone pair-statue of the Steward Memy-Sabu and his wife. This is the most successful of such rare compositions (*cf.* Plate 12) largely because the greater height of the man allows his left arm to be accommodated in a more natural pose. From Giza. Dynasty V–VI, *c.* 2340 B.C. Height 24 in. Metropolitan Museum, New York.

15 Painted limestone tomb-portal of the Palace Steward Iteti. This portion of a mastaba-chapel represents the doorway of a 'house of eternity' with the owner stepping forth to receive the offerings brought by pious relatives. A detailed list of such provisions is given on the jambs of the doorway. In the stela above, Iteti is shown seated before an altar on which are placed long slices of bread and a further list of funerary offerings. From Saqqara. Dynasty VI, *c.* 2330 B.C. Height 77 in. Cairo Museum.

16 Painted limestone relief from the mortuary temple of King Weser-kaf at Saqqara. This fragment is from a scene which would have shown the royal owner fowling in the marshes, a composition which survives in more complete versions in several private mastaba-chapels of the Old Kingdom. Here a hoopoe, ibis and other birds are among the papyrus thickets: over all, flutters a butterfly. From Saqqara. Early Dynasty V, *c.* 2490 B.C. Height 31 in. Cairo Museum.

17 Limestone relief from the Pyramid causeway of King Wenis at Saqqara, showing a group of Bedouin (?) men, women and children suffering from the dire effects of severe famine. Late Dynasty V, *c.* 2350 B.C.

18 Painted limestone relief in the mastaba-chapel of the Vizier and Governor of Memphis Mereruka at Saqqara, after the copy by the Oriental Institute, Chicago, showing work in the harvest field. In the upper register peasants load an ass with a large pannier for carrying the sheaves of corn while three companions struggle with the obstinate she-ass who refuses her burden. In the lower register reapers, with bags over their shoulders, cut the corn with sickles in unison to the sound of a flute. The hieroglyphic legends enshrine the banter of the workers, 'Where have you got to, you slow-coach?' and, 'This is fine barley, mate!' etc. Dynasty VI, *c.* 2380 B.C. Scale 1:8.

19 Copper altar and suite of ritual vessels belonging to the priest Idy. From Abydos. Dynasty VI, *c.* 2200 B.C. Length of altar 15½ in. British Museum, London.

20 Alabaster statuette of King Phiops I wearing the White Crown and a short cloak rising to a stand-off peak at the shoulders, carrying the crook and *ladanisterion* and seated upon a stark block throne. This is the image of the King-in-Jubilee (*i.e.* in resurrection) which is also adopted for representation of the god Osiris. It is customary to refer to such statues of the King as 'Osiride' (*cf.* Plates 56, 58) though to do so is to reverse the proper order. The figure of the hawk on the throne (*cf.* Plate 9) acts as a hieroglyph in the name inscribed on the back-pillar, but also symbolizes Horus, the living King, as opposed to his father Osiris, the resurrected King of the Dead. Perhaps from Saqqara. Dynasty VI, *c.* 2280 B.C. Height 10 in. Brooklyn Museum.

21 Painted wooden model of a company of forty Nubian archers found with a companion group of Egyptian spearmen. From the tomb of Mesehti at Asyut. Dynasty X, *c.* 2100 B.C. Height 14 in. Cairo Museum.

22 Painted wooden model of a funerary boat with the deceased represented as a mummy on a bier under a canopy, mourned by two priestesses

impersonating the divine weepers Isis and Nephthys, the sisters who mourned over their murdered brother Osiris. Such ship-models replace scenes in late Old Kingdom tombs showing the owner navigating on the waters of 'the Goodly West'. Length 26 in. British Museum, London.

23 Painted sandstone statue of King Menthu-hotep Neb-hepet-re in his white jubilee-robe wearing the Red Crown of Lower Egypt (*cf.* Plate 20). Excavated by Howard Carter from the cenotaph beneath the pyramid of the King's mortuary temple at Deir el-Bahri, Thebes. Dynasty XI, *c.* 2050 B.C. Height 72 in. Cairo Museum.

24 Relief of King Sesostris I carved on one face of a limestone pillar from a temple of the King demolished to form the foundations of a later building at Karnak (*cf.* Plate 25). The scene shows an incident in the jubilee celebrations when the King visited the shrines of the main gods of Egypt and was received by them as their son. Here Sesostris and Ptah of Memphis embrace within a shrine. Dynasty XII, *c.* 1940 B.C. Height 105 in. Cairo Museum.

25 Jubilee kiosk of King Sesostris I, recently rebuilt at Karnak from the limestone masonry excavated from the foundations of the Third Pylon at Thebes. This little temple is hypethral with a ramp at opposite ends. A podium in the central atrium probably supported two seated statues of Sesostris wearing jubilee costume and different crowns (*cf.* Plates 20, 23) but was adapted in the reign of Ammenemes III to act as a station for the barque of Amun. Dynasty XII, *c.* 1940 B.C.

In the background may be seen an alabaster shrine of Amenophis I, also recently reconstructed from the foundations of the same pylon, and used as a resting-place for the barque of Amun during its seasonal perambulations around Thebes (*cf.* Plate 53). Dynasty XVIII, *c.* 1535 B.C.

26 Relief of Queen Kawit, detail from one side of her limestone sarcophagus excavated by Edouard Naville from her pit-tomb in the funerary monument of Menthu-hotep I at Deir el-Bahri (see Fig. 37). The scene shows Kawit, mirror in hand, having her hair dressed by a maid, while her

steward encourages her to refresh herself with a cup of milk drawn from her cows in an adjoining relief. Early Dynasty XI, *c.* 2070 B.C. Height (of detail) 15 in. Cairo Museum.

27   Pectoral of the Princess Sit-Hathor-Yunet, gold, chased and engraved and inlaid with carnelian, turquoise and lapis lazuli, part of a hoard excavated by Petrie and Brunton at Lahun. The design is in the form of an elaborate rebus expressing the wish that the sun-god may grant an eternity of life to Sesostris II, the father of the princess. Dynasty XII, *c.* 1885 B.C. Height 1¾ in. Metropolitan Museum, New York.

28   Green glazed faience statuette of a hippopotamus decorated in line with the marsh plants among which it lurks. The plastic qualities of this piece owe much to the fact that it was modelled, not carved. Such figurines are peculiar to Middle Kingdom burials in which they may have served as amulets to protect the tomb or assist the rebirth of the dead man as a living spirit. Dynasty XII, *c.* 1880 B.C. Length 7½ in. Collection of Mr and Mrs R. J. Sainsbury, London.

29   Green chlorite (?) head of a queen from a rare representation of a female sphinx, a creature which in Egypt usually personified the Pharaoh. This antiquity was removed to Rome in Imperial times and was probably excavated at the site of Hadrian's villa at Tivoli in 1771 when it was acquired by Gavin Hamilton for Lord Shelburne. Dynasty XII, *c.* 1895 B.C. Height 15¼ in. Brooklyn Museum.

30   Black granite statue of King Sesostris II excavated by Auguste Mariette at Tanis, whence it had been carried off by Ramesses II (see Plate 55) who usurped it by cutting his ugly cartouches on it and adding the pectoral unfeelingly to the chest. Dynasty XII, *c.* 1880 B.C. Height 104 in. Cairo Museum.

31   Detail from a hard green stone statuette of Sesostris III acquired by Henry Salt, the British Consul in Egypt from 1816 to 1827 and sold by him with his second collection to the French Government through the persuasion of Champollion. It is incomplete, its provenance unknown, and until recently it was described as dating to the Saite period (*c.* 664–525

B.C.). Its proper identity has had to be established by stylistic means. Dynasty XII, *c.* 1870 B.C. Height 8¾ in. The Louvre, Paris.

32 Red quartzite head of a statue of an unknown man. The portraiture of this private person follows closely the fashion of contemporary royal statues and has no individuality, as is the usual custom at most periods in Egypt. Dynasty XII, *c.* 1870 B.C. Height 4⅛ in. Royal Scottish Museum, Edinburgh.

33 Upper part of a black granite statue of Ammenemes III excavated by Auguste Mariette at Mit Faris in the Faiyum. The King is shown wearing a bandolier, leopard-skin robe, and heavy wig perhaps originally surmounted by a feather, and carries two hawk-headed staves. This priestly garb may have had special significance for the predominantly Libyan inhabitants of the Faiyum. Dynasty XII, *c.* 1840 B.C. Height 39 in. Cairo Museum.

34 Painted limestone relief-fragment from the inner chambers of the tomb of Queen Neferu showing two of her retainers carrying her jewellery caskets and wig-boxes in the funeral procession. The relief is in the archaic Theban style of the early years of Menthu-hotep I (*cf.* Plate 26). From Deir el-Bahri, Thebes. Dynasty XI, *c.* 2060 B.C. Height 5½ in. Royal Scottish Museum, Edinburgh.

35 Wall-painting in the tomb of Khnum-hotep at Beni Hasan, after the copy of Nina M. Davies. Scale, 1:4. Part of a visiting group of Semites trading eye-paint with Khnum-hotep who was Governor of the Eastern Desert. The four women are preceded by a boy carrying a spear. They wear bright woven garments and leather boots. Their characteristic aquiline noses have been faithfully rendered. Dynasty XII, *c.* 1900 B.C.

36 Head of a parade axe of King Ahmosis, found in the coffin of his mother at Thebes and excavated by Mariette's agents. The axe-head is of copper overlaid with gold and electrum and inlaid with carnelian and blue and green frit. The scene shows the King despatching a native rebel and may have been given to him to celebrate a notable victory over a Hyksos collaborator. The war-god Menthu is shown below as a hawk-headed

sphinx with distinctly Helladic features. Such elaborate weapons were awarded to the King's officers for meritorious service in the field through-out the dynasty. Dynasty XVIII, *c.* 1570 B.C. Length 5¼ in. Cairo Museum.

37 The fortress at Buhen below the Second Cataract showing the north-west line of Middle Kingdom fortifications after the removal of later additions and reconstructions. The massive brick walls were over 15 ft high and strengthened by bastions. The foot of the wall was protected by a rampart with a loop-holed parapet overhanging the scarp of a rock-cut ditch more than 20 ft deep. Dynasty XII, *c.* 1990–1786 B.C.

38 The mortuary temple of Queen Hatshepsut at Deir el-Bahri, Western Thebes. Designed on the lines of the neighbouring temple of Menthu-hotep I (Fig. 37), but dispensing with the pyramid in the forecourt, this structure consists of two deep terraces within a large walled enclosure. A central ramp leads above the lower colonnade to the first terrace where a second ramp admits to the upper terrace with its central sanctuary cut in the cliff behind and dedicated to Amun. Within the double colonnades are bas-reliefs commemorating the Queen's birth, coronation and mighty works (see Fig. 37). Dynasty XVIII, *c.* 1480 B.C.

39 Hard limestone statue of Queen Hatshepsut, the body acquired at Thebes by Richard Lepsius in 1845 and the head and other fragments excavated by the Metropolitan Museum Expedition in 1926–8 and rejoined as the result of an exchange. Though this statue, which may have been destined for the inner sanctuary of the temple, shows the Queen in all the trappings of a Pharaoh, full justice is done to her femininity in the idealistic manner of the dynasty. Dynasty XVIII, *c.* 1480 B.C. Height 77 in. Metropolitan Museum, New York.

40 Dark granite statue of Sennemut and the Princess Neferu-re. Sennemut, the chief architect of Hatshepsut, began his career as a soldier in the armies of Tuthmosis I, the Queen's father, and rose to be her steward and favourite. He is seen here as the tutor of the young Princess Neferu-re who is represented as a child wearing a sidelock and putting her finger in her mouth (*cf.* Plate 72). From Thebes. Dynasty XVIII, *c.* 1480 B.C. Height 28 in. British Museum, London.

41   Grey basalt statue of King Tuthmosis III excavated by Georges Legrain
from a great cache of temple sculpture at Karnak. The complete statue
shows the great conqueror wearing the White Crown and treading upon
nine bows symbolizing the hereditary foreign subjects of the King. This
portrait head is a close, if idealized, likeness of the King as his mummy
shows. Dynasty XVIII, *c.* 1460 B.C. Height 79 in. Cairo Museum.

42   Black basalt statue-head of Amenophis III as a young king during his
early reign. The large almond eyes, the geometrically arched eye-brows
and the upturned corners of the lips reveal that stylization and tendency
to abstraction that creeps into the official art of this reign as the Pharaoh
becomes more of a god than a conqueror. Through a misreading of one
of his names, the Greeks identified him with their Homeric Memnon.
Height 24 in. Brooklyn Museum.

43   House of the Vizier Nakht at Amarna. View, taken soon after its excavation by the British, from the Central Hall which was over 30 ft
square. A stone lustration slab and splash-back can be seen in an inner
reception room. The walls and floor were of mud-brick, the red-painted
wooden columns were supported on the circular stone bases seen in the
foreground. A similar base in the inner room is obscured by a brick
hearth. Dynasty XVIII, *c.* 1360 B.C.

44   Green schistose statue-head of Queen Tiy excavated by Flinders Petrie
in a temple-ruin in Sinai. This little head of the chief wife of Amenophis
III with its pouting expression seems to reveal a more realistic approach
to portraiture than does most of the idealistic statuary of the reign. Tiy
was not of royal blood but the daughter of the King's Lieutenant of
Chariotry. Dynasty XVIII, *c.* 1375 B.C. Height 3½ in. Cairo Museum.

45   Plaster mask of a man excavated by Ludwig Borchardt in the ruins of a
sculptor's studio at Amarna. As well as carved sculptures, two kinds of
plaster casts were also found, those so naturalistic in handling that they
have been identified as life or death masks, and those displaying all the
conventions of contemporary stone sculpture. It has been plausibly suggested that the former group into which this specimen falls, are probably
sculptors' studies, modelled rapidly in clay from the life and fixed by

casting. Thereafter such models would be worked on to produce an idealized likeness for copying in stone. Dynasty XVIII, *c.* 1350 B.C. Height 9½ in. Berlin Museum.

46 Upper part of a colossal sandstone statue of King Akhenaten from the site of the early temple to the Aten at Karnak. This extraordinary statue, one of several such colossi over 13 ft high, shows the King carrying sceptres, wearing a kerchief over a long wig more appropriate for a god, and bracelets and armlets inscribed with the name of the Aten. The emaciated features and peculiar physique of the King have been exag/gerated into a mannerism designed to accentuate the inhuman and there/fore god/like quality of the ruler. Such a revolutionary distortion could never have been devised by a court artist and must owe its origin to Akhenaten himself who, judging from the bones believed to be his, suffered from a pathological condition. Dynasty XVIII, *c.* 1368 B.C. Cairo Museum.

47 Alabaster ointment/spoon with the handle in the form of a swimming girl, her hair and girdle of dark slate inlays. She supports a pet gazelle, the hollowed/out body of which forms the container for the unguent, the upper part swivelling as a lid. Such charming toilet objects are charac/teristic of the luxurious Amarna Period. Dynasty XVIII, *c.* 1370 B.C. Length 9 in. Metropolitan Museum, New York.

48 Portion of the rear panel of a throne from the tomb of King Tut/ankh/amun. This relief is carved in wood overlaid with gold and silver and inlaid with brilliant blue faience and coloured opaque glass. It shows the third daughter of Akhenaten, Queen Ankhes/en/amun annointing her husband during his coronation ceremonies, for which he wears the triple Atefu crown. The rays of the Aten bring the symbols of life to the nostrils of the royal couple (*cf.* Fig. 4). Dynasty XVIII, *c.* 1352. Height 9 in. Cairo Museum.

49 Black granite statue of the Scribe of Recruits, Amenophis/son/of/Hapu shown seated cross/legged about to write on the papyrus/roll open on his lap: his head is bowed in reverence before the unseen god who inspires his words. From Karnak. Dynasty XVIII, *c.* 1370 B.C. Height 51 in. Cairo Museum.

50 Grey granite statue of the General Haremhab shown not as a warrior but a military scribe writing a long hymn to Thoth, the god of learning (*cf.* Plate 49). The statue was made for Haremhab while he was still holding high office, but not yet king, and set up in the temple of Ptah at Memphis, on which site it was found. Dynasty XVIII, *c.* 1345 B.C. Height 46 in. Metropolitan Museum, New York.

51 Wall-painting from the tomb of the Chief Treasurer, Sobek-hotep, at Thebes; after the copy by Nina M. Davies. Syrians, accompanied by young children, are shown bringing gold and silver vessels, an oil-horn and a quiver as gifts to the Pharaoh at his accession. The last bearer in the lower register carries an eagle-headed rhyton upon a bowl, an object of Minoan design, perhaps acquired by trade with the Aegean. Dynasty XVIII, *c.* 1390 B.C. Height 44 in. British Museum, London.

52 Wall-painting in the tomb of the Scribe of Crown Lands, Menna, at Thebes; after the copy by Nina M. Davies. In the lower register left, Menna sits under a light canopy while a steward reports on the harvest. Reapers cut the corn with sickles under the direction of a scribe; one pauses to take a pull at a jar. In the background, under an acacia, one of the woman gleaners feeds from a bowl of fruit while her child slung around in a shawl plays with her hair (*cf.* Plate 80). In the upper register Menna's chariot and groom wait while the scribes measure and record the amount of threshed grain. Dynasty XVIII, *c.* 1390 B.C. Height 30 in.

53 Unfinished limestone stela with the ink-drawing in its final form but awaiting the sculptor's chisel. The upper register shows the barque of Amun of Thebes with its ram's-head ornaments at prow and stern borne in procession on carrying-poles during some Theban festival by twenty priests like the Ark of the Covenant. Beside it walks the First Prophet in his leopard-skin robe. Below, the scribe of the necropolis, Amun-nakhte, his son and brother offer a prayer to the god. From Deir el-Medina, Thebes. Dynasty XX, *c.* 1170 B.C. Metropolitan Museum, New York.

54 Painted limestone relief in the temple of King Sethos I at Abydos, showing the King at his Coronation carrying sceptres, wearing the elaborate Atefu crown (*cf.* Plates 48, 72), and supported on his throne by

the Lower Egyptian Edjo of Buto and the Upper Egyptian Nekhebet of el-Kab, both in the guise of elegant goddesses and not in their more usual cobra and vulture forms. Dynasty XIX, *c.* 1303 B.C. Scale, 1:8.

55 Black granite statue of King Ramesses II wearing contemporary dress instead of the more usual traditional garb (*cf.* Plates 12, 30). The figure of the queen by his left leg, and that of his son by his right leg, appear on a greatly reduced scale (*cf.* Plates 13, 57). From the prenomen of this King the Greek form *Ozymandias* of Diodorus (and Shelley) was derived. From Thebes. Dynasty XIX, *c.* 1290 B.C. Height 76 in. Turin Museum.

56 Osiride statues in the ruined second court of the 'Ramesseum' at Thebes. In this mortuary temple of Ramesses II, the dead King is identified with the god Osiris. The cliffs of Western Thebes can be seen in the background, honeycombed with the tombs of the royal officials. Dynasty XIX, *c.* 1250 B.C.

57 Façade of the larger temple of Ramesses II at Abu Simbel in Lower Nubia. The temple is hewn out of the sandstone cliff to a distance of 180 ft. The four seated colossi, over 60 ft high, represent the King with members of his family, carved on a smaller scale, by his legs. The temple is dedicated primarily to the sun-god, and it is so orientated that at sunrise a shaft of light strikes into the innermost sanctuary, animating the statues of the gods and the king. The inside walls are adorned with reliefs of the king's warlike exploits. The first European travellers in 1812 and 1817 found the temple almost buried in sand-drifts and the first notable clearance was made by Mariette in 1869, when it was visited in moonlight by the Empress Eugénie and her suite. Graffiti of all periods have been added by visitors, from the Lydian and Carian mercenaries of Psammetichos II (*c.* 590 B.C.) to the British soldiers who defeated a force of dervishes near-by in 1889. Dynasty XIX, *c.* 1250 B.C.

58 Lid of the red granite sarcophagus of King Ramesses III, surmounted by the recumbent effigy of the King represented as Osiris mourned and supported on either side by the figures of the goddesses Isis and Nephthys (*cf.* Plate 22). The body of this sarcophagus is in the Louvre. From the King's tomb at Thebes. Dynasty XX, *c.* 1150 B.C. Length 118 in. Fitzwilliam Museum, Cambridge.

59 Painted sunk relief carved on the exterior rear south wall of the First Pylon of the mortuary temple of Ramesses III at Medinet Habu, Western Thebes: after the copy by the Oriental Institute, Chicago. The King is shown in his chariot despatching wounded wild cattle in a payprus thicket on the bank of a stream. His sons hunt on foot with bow and arrow. An escort of soldiers acts as beaters. Dynasty XX, *c.* 1150 B.C. Scale, 1:60.

60 Detail of painted sunk relief carved on the interior rear east wall of the Second Pylon of the mortuary temple of Ramesses III at Medinet Habu, Western Thebes, showing dead and dying Libyan foemen. Dynasty XX, *c.* 1150 B.C. Scale, 1:10. After the copy by the Oriental Institute, Chicago.

61 Wall-painting in the tomb of the sculptor Ipy at Deir el-Medina, Western Thebes; after the copy by Norman de G. Davies. Workmen are putting the finishing touches to a tabernacle used in the cult of the long-dead king, Amenophis I, the patron of the Theban necropolis. On the roof of the shrine carpenters cut mortices and smooth down woodwork with stone rubbers; another wakes a sleeping comrade as the surveyor approaches. On the left, the foreman shouts up directions, while below him an itinerant eye-doctor touches up the visage of a carpenter with kohl. Dynasty XIX, *c.* 1280 B.C. Scale, 1:5.

62 Limestone *ostrakon* with a coloured drawing of a female tumbler of a kind who performed in certain religious festivals. From Deir el-Medina, Western Thebes. Dynasty XIX–XX, *c.* 1180 B.C. Length $6\frac{5}{8}$ in. Turin Museum.

63 Painted wooden shawabti-figure of King Ramesses IV, inscribed with the magic spell for causing the substitute to do all the work of the con-scribed labourer in the Osirian hereafter. From the tomb of the King, Thebes. Dynasty XX, *c.* 1141 B.C. Height 10 in. The Louvre, Paris.

64–6 Polychrome faience tiles from Thebes, similar to others found in the ruins of the Delta Residences of the Ramessides, and made to be set into plas-tered mud-brick walls. Plain blue tiles containing the titularies of the kings in white glyphs were used as framing for doorways and balconies. Of the traditional captive foes of the Pharaoh, No. 64 represents a Syrian in his gaudy robes, and No. 65 a negro with large ear-ring and panther-skin kilt. No. 66 is part of a frieze with designs of lapwings squatting on baskets with arms upraised, symbolizing the people of Egypt adoring their ruler. Dynasty XX, *c.* 1150 B.C. Average height 10 in. Museum of Fine Arts, Boston.

67 Green schistose statue of the High Priest of Amun, Ramesses-nakht kneeling to present a small shrine surmounted by the Theban triad—Amun, his consort Mut, and their son Khons, the moon-god. Ramesses-nakht, and two of his sons who succeeded him in turn, greatly increased the power of the priesthood of Amun during the reigns of the later Ramessides. From the cache at Karnak (*cf.* Plate 41). Dynasty XX, *c.* 1120 B.C. Height 12 in. Cairo Museum.

68 Blue-glazed faience footed cup, one of a small group of such vessels in the form of a half-opened lotus-flower, in which the decoration is skilfully modelled in relief on the thin walls. In this example the main design shows an unnamed Pharaoh smiting the state enemies (*cf.* Plate 5). Dynasty XXII, *c.* 900 B.C. Height 6¼ in. Myers Collection, Eton College, Windsor.

69 Gold funerary mask of King Psusennes I from his mummy discovered by Pierre Montet in a secondary burial at Tanis in 1940. While this life-sized mask lacks the opulence and artistic excellence of a similar inlaid helmet mask found on the body of Tut-ankh-amun, it still reveals a high standard of craftsmanship and luxury in the royal funerary furnishings. Dynasty XXI, *c.* 1000 B.C. Cairo Museum.

70 Gold statuette, cast solid, of the god Amun of Thebes, shown 'wide of stride' holding a scimitar in one hand and the symbol of life in the other. The tall plumes that surmounted his characteristic cap (*cf.* Plate 67) were torn off by the *sebakhin* who unearthed this and another gold object in the ruins of an ancient city, perhaps Bubastis. Dynasty XXII, *c.* 900 B.C. Height 7 in. Metropolitan Museum, New York.

71 Bronze statue of Queen Karomama made for her chapel at Karnak by the priest of Amun and official of the Divine Consorts, Ah-tef-nakht.

The details of the floral collar and embroidered dress, with its elaborate feather-pattern, were inlaid with gold, silver and electrum. A crown and two plumes, doubtless of gold, surmounted the coiffure (*cf.* Plate 75), and the hands originally held sistra or sceptres probably of gold. This statue was bought by Champollion during his mission to Egypt in 1829 and was immediately recognized by him as the most beautiful object of its kind known, a judgement which time has not altered. Dynasty XXII, *c.* 825 B.C. Height 20½ in. The Louvre, Paris.

72 Green-glazed faience relief of King Yewepet. This plaque, and its companion piece in the Brooklyn Museum, are all that is left of a shrine at Thebes of this little-known king who was defeated by the Khushite Pi-ankhy, *c.* 720 B.C. Yewepet is shown here as the child-king Horus, finger in mouth, wearing the triple Atefu crown of a newly enthroned king. The lotus on which he squats represents the remote marsh-lands in which he was reared by his mother Isis after the murder of her husband Osiris. Such representations are usual for very youthful kings and those whose claims were not perhaps very strong. Dynasty XXIII, *c.* 725 B.C. Height 12 in. Royal Scottish Museum, Edinburgh.

73 Black granite statue-head of King Tarhaqa showing him wearing the rough-surfaced skull-cap favoured by the 'Ethiopian' monarchs. His Nubian features are rendered with all the high technical brilliance of the 'new art' revived at Thebes under Menthu-em-het. From Luxor. Dynasty XXV, *c.* 670 B.C. Height 14 in. Cairo Museum.

74 Detail of a dark granite statue of the Fourth Prophet of Amun Menthu-em-het who as the High Steward of the Divine Consort of Amun (*cf.* Plate 75) was a great patron of the new art of the time which drew its inspiration from the masterpieces of the past. This statue displays the remarkable eclecticism characteristic of this art. The pose and costume of the statue are in the tradition of the Old Kingdom, but the searching portraiture is inspired by Middle Kingdom royal statuary (*cf.* Plates 31, 33). The wig copies a New Kingdom fashion (*cf.* Plate 49). From the cache at Karnak (*cf.* Plate 41). Dynasty XXV, *c.* 660 B.C. Height (complete) 61 in. Cairo Museum.

75 Ivory statuette of a Divine Consort of Amun, probably Amenirdas the sister of King Piʻankhy. Such human partners of an intangible god wore all the habit and crowns of a chief wife of the Pharaoh and virtually ruled the Thebaid during the late Libyan, Ethiopian and Saitic dynasties. They adopted their successors from among the daughters of the Pharaoh. Dynasty XXV, *c.* 660 B.C. Height 8 in. Royal Scottish Museum, Edinburgh.

76 Black basaltic stone statueʻhead of King Apries, the Hophra of Jeremiah, who became unpopular for the privileges he bestowed upon Greek traders and soldiers. After two disastrous defeats in Phoenicia and Cyrene, he was deposed by his army in favour of Amasis, and murdered three years later during a revolt. Perhaps from Sais. Dynasty XXVI, *c.* 580 B.C. Height 15¾ in. Bologna Museum.

77 Quartzite sandstone statueʻhead of King Amasis, the General of the army who overthrew Apries and ruled in his stead. During his long reign, he was able by means of a strong fleet to control the coasts of the Levant and capture Cyprus. At the end of his prosperous reign, the rising power of Persia threatened trouble which broke in the first year of his successor. Perhaps from Sais. Dynasty XXVI, *c.* 550 B.C. Height 16 in. University Museum, Philadelphia.

78 Limestone relief from the tomb of the Governor of Upper Egypt Nesʻpekaʻshuti at Thebes. The mannerist abstractions of Late Period art are well illustrated in this relief. The gestures and ungirt bosoms show that the figures represent mourning women, both young and old, in the manner of the weepers in New Kingdom scenes, but little emotion is displayed either by pose or facial expression. The artist has been more concerned with the rhythms and patterns created by the upʻraised hands, the tied girdles and the sausageʻlike coiffures, than with conveying the idea of grief. Dynasty XXVI, *c.* 650 B.C. Length 19½ in. Brooklyn Museum.

79 Portion of limestone wall from the tomb of the Fourth Prophet of Amun, Menthuʻemʻhet, at Thebes, showing a version in bas relief of a unique scene painted in the tomb of Menna of over 700 years earlier. The relief

is more elegant in its careful details (*cf.* Plate 52), but the source of inspiration is undoubted. In the remains of the upper register may be identified another unique tableau from the same tomb where two girl gleaners pause while one removes a thorn from her companion's foot. Dynasty XXV, *c.* 660 B.C. Length 11¼ in. Brooklyn Museum.

80   Detail from a black basalt fragment of stela in the form of a shrine carved in high relief with figures of two officials, father and son, wearing sleeved garments of Persian pattern. The carving of the features attempts to distinguish between youth and age. Probably from Sais. Dynasty XXVII, *c.* 520 B.C. Width 6½ in. Royal Scottish Museum, Edinburgh.

81   Green schist statue-head of a man. From Thebes. Late Period, *c.* 4th century B.C. Height 6 in. Brooklyn Museum.

82   Entrance gate in the pylon of the temple of the hawk and sun-god Horus at Edfu, with the main court beyond leading to the vestibule and inner halls. The history of the building under most of the Ptolemies is inscribed at length on its girdle wall. The deep channels on either side of the gate were for the reception of tall flag-poles. Mariette, who first cleared the temple from encroaching rubbish, also had to remove a whole Arab village from its roof. Ptolemaic Period, 237–57 B.C.

Index

The Egyptians